CW01311015

# Dark Psychology

*What Machiavellian People of Power Know about Persuasion, Mind Control, Manipulation, Negotiation, Deception, Human Behavior, and Psychological Warfare that You Don't*

# Contents

INTRODUCTION ..................................................................................... 1
CHAPTER 1: MACHIAVELLIAN POWER ........................................... 3
    FAMOUS MACHIAVELLIAN LEADERS ................................................... 4
    THE EIGHT TRAITS OF MACHIAVELLIAN POWER ................................ 4
    PROTECTING YOURSELF FROM MACHIAVELLIAN POWERS ................. 7
CHAPTER 2: THE EIGHT LAWS OF HUMAN BEHAVIOR ..................... 8
    PEOPLE ACCEPT RECOGNITION AND AVOID ACCOUNTABILITY .......... 9
    PEOPLE DO THINGS FOR THEIR OWN REASONS, NOT OURS .............. 12
    PEOPLE RARELY CHANGE THEIR MINDS EVEN THOUGH THEY ARE PROVEN WRONG .......................................................................................... 16
    PEOPLE MAKE DECISIONS BASED ON EMOTION AND JUSTIFY THEM WITH FACTS ............................................................................................ 19
    PEOPLE WANT TO FEEL IN CONTROL OF THEIR LIVES ..................... 22
    PEOPLE WANT TO BE PART OF SOMETHING LARGER THAN THEMSELVES ........ 26
    PEOPLE WANT TO BE TREATED AS UNIQUE OR SPECIAL .................. 34
CHAPTER 3: THE SIX SCIENTIFIC PRINCIPLES OF PERSUASION .... 38
    RECIPROCITY ....................................................................................... 39
    SCARCITY ............................................................................................. 40
    AUTHORITY .......................................................................................... 41
    CONSISTENCY ...................................................................................... 41

LIKING ............................................................................................................. 42

CONSENSUS ...................................................................................................... 43

**CHAPTER 4: CLEVER MIND CONTROL TECHNIQUES ......................... 44**

FLOODING SMILE ............................................................................................. 45

MAKE ANYONE LIKE YOU ............................................................................. 45

REPEAT YOURSELF ......................................................................................... 46

SYNCHRONIZED ACTIVITIES ........................................................................ 46

BE QUIET ........................................................................................................... 46

RANSBERGER PIVOT ...................................................................................... 47

TELL A LIE ........................................................................................................ 47

CONTROL THE CONVERSATION .................................................................. 48

PERFECT NOD .................................................................................................. 48

THE EYES .......................................................................................................... 49

**CHAPTER 5: TECHNIQUES FROM THE BEST NEGOTIATORS ........... 50**

WE ARE NOT DRIVEN BY REASON ............................................................. 51

DON'T FEEL SOMEONE'S PAIN, LABEL IT ................................................. 52

USE THE WORDS "YOU'RE RIGHT" ............................................................. 54

BEND SOMEONE'S REALITY ........................................................................ 54

CREATE AN ILLUSION OF CONTROL ......................................................... 55

GUARANTEE EXECUTION ............................................................................. 56

DRIVE A HARD BARGAIN ............................................................................. 56

**CHAPTER 6: 19 PREDATORY MANIPULATION TECHNIQUES ........... 58**

LYING ................................................................................................................ 59

MOOD SWINGS ................................................................................................ 61

LOVE BOMBING AND DEVALUATION ...................................................... 62

DENIAL .............................................................................................................. 64

SPINNING THE TRUTH ................................................................................... 65

MINIMIZING ..................................................................................................... 66

PLAYING THE VICTIM ................................................................................... 67

Using Positive Reinforcement ................................................................. 68
  Moving the Goal Posts ........................................................................... 69
  Diversion ................................................................................................... 70
  Sarcasm .................................................................................................... 71
  Guilt Tripping ......................................................................................... 71
  Flattery ................................................................................................... 72
  Playing Innocent ................................................................................... 73
  Excessive Aggression ........................................................................... 74
  Isolation ................................................................................................. 75
  They Fake Love and Empathy ............................................................. 77
**CHAPTER 7: DECEPTIVE WINNERS** ............................................. **78**
  Deceive People about your Resources ............................................. 78
  Deceive People into Believing in your Strategy ............................ 80
  Deception Is a Tool Not a Plan .......................................................... 81
  Use Deception to Cover your Tracks ................................................ 82
**CONCLUSION** ............................................................................................ **84**

# Introduction

If you have ever been manipulated in your life, the chances are that you know exactly what it is like to be subjected to the painful and damaging behaviors of people who seem to lack morals. You may find yourself wondering what could possibly compel a person to behave in such a destructive manner, or how they even do it in the first place. While the reasons that contribute to someone's destructive and damaging behaviors are extensive, the strategies they use to accomplish their destruction are fairly straightforward. They rely on tools like manipulation, deception, negotiation, mind control, human behavior, and psychological warfare to get their way.

The contents of this book will help you develop a deeper understanding of the tools that have been used in dark psychology to help people achieve what is commonly known as "Machiavellian power". This form of power is dark, destructive, and often comes at the expense of many good people who were unknowingly and unintentionally dragged into the games of the deceptive leader. In the end, it's often the Machiavellian leader who lacks empathy and compassion towards others that wins; thus making it easy for them to serve up dishes of torture, destruction, and pain with zero remorse for their actions or behaviors.

By educating yourself on what these types of behaviors are and how they work, you can protect yourself from being deceived by a Machiavellian power. The more you understand how these twisted games work and accept the fact that a Machiavellian has no moral compass or empathy for those around them, the easier it becomes to identify their behaviors and protect yourself from their destruction. In some cases, being involved with them may be completely inevitable, such as if they are your boss or a person in politics who rules over your country. However, understanding their tactics and strategies can prevent you from being sucked into their destruction and, hopefully, ensure that you remain sound of mind so that you can avoid the mental torture and pain that comes from their behaviors. Please note that this book is in no way intended to endorse manipulative behaviors or encourage dark psychological tools like deception and mind control. Instead, it is meant to educate you so that you can protect yourself against these destructive behaviors.

If you are ready to discover how Machiavellians work and understand how you can protect yourself against their deceptive and dangerous strategies, then it is time to begin! Please, take your time reading this book as there is much to be learned on this subject and it can be quite challenging to read if you are still recovering from the destruction of a manipulator.

# Chapter 1: Machiavellian Power

Machiavellian power is a form of power used by individuals who employ cunning and duplicity as a means to achieve control over others. It arose in the mid-1400s from the Italian Renaissance diplomat and writer Niccolò Machiavelli who was famous for many of his writings, such as *Il Principe* (*The Prince*) Nowadays, Machiavellianism is a word that is used to describe one of the dark triad personality types that people employ, allowing them to express a cynical disregard for morality so that they can focus on personal gain.

Machiavellian power is a form of power that is derived from individuals who can completely dissociate from their emotions and morals to achieve selfish gains. Through this detachment, they can manipulate others in a highly powerful way, duping them into faithfully following the powerful Machiavellian individual, often without even realizing that they are doing so. The ways of Machiavellianism are so dark and twisted that often people with good hearts and kind souls fail to understand that such a dark and twisted power could even exist. Frequently, they are sucked into believing anything that the cynical individual says and find themselves genuinely believing that they are contributing something positive to the world around them.

People who identify with Machiavellianism genuinely believe that the world is a selfish and evil place. They believe in statements like "Never tell anyone the real reason you did something unless it is useful to do so," but they do not believe in statements like "Most people are good and kind." Machiavellians are motivated by selfishness and have a strong ability to manipulate others. They also tend to be extremely intelligent on the intelligent quotient (IQ) scale but frequently score lower on the emotional quotient (EQ) scale. It is believed that their high intelligence is used to increase their manipulative abilities and their low emotional intelligence supports them in detaching from morals and emotions like empathy and compassion for others.

## Famous Machiavellian Leaders

Some of the most famous Machiavellian leaders throughout history include those like Shakespeare's Julius Caesar, Louis XI of France, Catherine de' Medici, Otto von Bismarck, François Mitterrand, and Félix Houphouët-Boigny. Each of these leaders was known to employ the lessons taught by Niccolò Machiavelli in his writings, using them as a means to gain control over the masses and lead in extremely selfish ways. Often, their leadership was built around helping themselves live incredible lives without giving much regard to the quality of lives being lived by those around them.

## The Eight Traits of Machiavellian Power

Eight traits characterize those who engage in Machiavellian power. Not all individuals who employ Machiavellian power will have all of these traits, but they will have at least a few of them and will likely use them on a regular basis.

The eight Machiavellian power traits are:

*Duplicity*

Machiavellian leaders are known for being duplicitous. They will act as one person to your face yet they will be another person behind your back. Rarely will a Machiavellian person show their true colors or ever reveal or express themselves to anyone, not even those who are closest to them. The only person who knows who they truly are is themselves, and even then, they likely do not have a strong grasp of their own identity.

## Cunningness

Machiavellian leaders are known for being extremely talented in getting what they want and regularly create masterpieces. Their success is typically the result of a crafty combination of trickery and wiliness.

## Narcissism

Virtually every Machiavellian is a narcissist. Their narcissism is likely how they can detach from things like empathy and compassion because they likely never experience it in the first place. Machiavellian leaders, like narcissists, have an exaggerated sense of self-importance, even if they often portray themselves as noble and humble. At the end of the day, this is just an example of their duplicitous behavior.

## Believes the Ends Justify the Means

A Machiavellian leader believes that as long as the outcome is desirable, there is nothing too unreasonable to achieve the said outcome. Machiavellians have been known to murder, imprison, and torture individuals who stand in their way, often doing so in secret and without ever getting caught in the act. They are also not above employing someone else to do their dirty work for them so that they are not caught or held responsible for their actions.

## Believes Everyone is Part of Their Game

Machiavellian leaders do not see people as individuals; instead, they see people as pawns in their game. To them, other individuals do not have feelings or values to be considered. They are not even seen as human. Every interaction that a Machiavellian leader engages in, from their workplace to their family life and anywhere in between, is all a part of a game to them. In this game, their only objective is to either gain or maintain their power or their influence over others.

*Excels in Control and Manipulation*

One of the key ways that Machiavellian leaders gain their control is through manipulation. Machiavellian leaders are known for manipulating and controlling others as a means to get anything they want any time they want it. The thing about their manipulation tactics is that, in many cases, people do not even realize that they are being manipulated. For the most part, they believe that they are doing the right thing or that they have made the choice to act in accordance with the Machiavellian leader on their own accord. In reality, it was all perfectly orchestrated by the Machiavellian leader.

*Would Rather be Feared than Loved*

Like anyone, a Machiavellian leader wants to be loved by others; the idea of being loved by others feels good to them. In many cases, their entire plot to the top is based on their desire to have everyone love them. Unfortunately, to a Machiavellian, being loved and being feared (or "respected") are synonymous. Machiavellians do not understand what true love is, nor do they know what it feels like to have people willingly feel love for them because they are too busy pressuring everyone into fearing them and manipulating them into believing that such fear *is* a sign of love. A Machiavellian leader will never say that they would prefer to be feared out loud though. Instead, they say that they want to be respected and lead other people into believing that their fear is a sign of respect.

*Does Not Reveal Their True Motivations*

A Machiavellian leader will never reveal their true motivations, not even to those around them or who are close to them. Even if you are working alongside a Machiavellian, they will never explain to you what they truly want to gain. The people around the Machiavellian leader often find themselves doing things for the leader without ever fully understanding why or how it contributes to the overall cause. This is because they never know exactly what the cause is. The only time a Machiavellian will reveal their true motivations or reasons is if it will, in some way, become advantageous to them. If it won't, they will not speak.

## Protecting Yourself from Machiavellian Powers

Protecting yourself from the powers of dark psychology, like Machiavellian power, comes from understanding what these types of powers look like. For many, the belief that someone could be so cold and shameless seems too unrealistic. They simply do not believe that anyone could behave so immorally. The reality is that many people lead with a Machiavellian rule, even in today's world. While not all will go so far as to commit physical crimes against others to increase their personal gain, they will certainly call on psychological warfare to improve their ability to achieve their own end game.

Machiavellian leaders can be your boss, a family member, a political person or virtually anyone else that you may encounter in your day-to-day life. There is no visual evidence that someone is Machiavellian. They often go under the radar and are never fully exposed for who they are. This is why many people find themselves getting duped by Machiavellian people without ever having realized what happened. If you want to avoid getting duped by a Machiavelli, you need to understand exactly what it is that they do, the tactics they use, and what these tactics look like. This is what we are going to explore as we dig deeper into human behavior, manipulation, mind control, persuasion, negotiation, deception, and psychological warfare.

# Chapter 2: The Eight Laws of Human Behavior

Human behavior is a fairly complex thing, but it is typically driven by eight laws. These laws outline the motivations behind most people's behaviors and actions and what it is that they are trying to achieve from everything that they do. They also help determine whether or not someone will do something based on how it falls within the laws of their behavior. For example, humans are driven by their need to know *why* they should do something, not *how*. Therefore, if you are attempting to sell something to someone, you need to explain why they should be interested, not how it will change their lives. This allows the individual to understand what they will gain and why it will change their lives, and then they can consider how the process actually works later on.

Machiavellian people are highly intelligent, so they know exactly what the eight laws of human behavior are, even if they have never gone out of their way to learn such information. Through watching, testing, and paying attention, Machiavellian leaders know how to identify these traits in people and use them as a means to manipulate their behavior and get what they want.

In this chapter, we are going to explore the eight laws of human behavior and how they work, as well as how people with power use these behaviors as an opportunity to manipulate others and get their way, often without ever getting noticed for their manipulative behaviors. As you read through these laws of behavior, notice how they appear in your own life and where these laws have motivated you. Then, consider how they can be used against you. By understanding these points in your behavior and recognizing them as being vulnerable towards masterful manipulators, you can lead your life with a greater sense of self-awareness and avoid being duped by a manipulator, such as a Machiavellian leader.

## People Accept Recognition and Avoid Accountability

People are known for being more than willing to accept recognition while avoiding responsibility. In doing so, they award themselves the opportunity to receive all the praise despite never having actually done anything to earn it. In most instances, the hard work was completed by others while they sat around and took credit anyway. We see this happen consistently all over the world, particularly with bosses and CEOs who rarely engage in the company work but take all of the credit for the success that the company produces. This is not just a phenomenon amongst corporations; it is a common influencer behind many people's behaviors.

To take recognition for things that have been done despite never having done any of the work means that you get to feel good more often than not. Even amongst children, we frequently see one child actually accomplishing something and another child taking responsibility for the said accomplishments, such as during school group work. In these situations, the child is being motivated by the recognition but is pushing everyone else to do the work for them so that they do not actually have to do anything to receive the recognition. Often, this is not done with the desire to be malicious or deceptive, but instead, we allow it to happen because the process of being recognized feels good.

The chances are that you can easily recognize this behavior in your own life for things that you have done. For example, maybe you started a new hobby or business venture and accepted the praises of those who said that you were brave and talented, but when it came time to seeing the hobby or venture through, you stopped putting in the effort, and everything fell apart. In situations like these, it can be easy to say that it was a lack of motivation or drive that resulted in you not seeing it through and you can naturally move on to the next thing and continue with your life. However, that is not always the case.

People who are manipulative are known to use this as an opportunity to increase their personal gains at the expense of others around them. A famous case of this happening was in the interactions that took place between Thomas Edison and Nikola Tesla when electricity and other primitive electronic devices were being developed more than 100 years ago. In this exchange, Edison had hired Tesla to work for him, requiring Tesla to work for 18 hours a day to fulfill his job duties. At one point, Edison proposed that if Tesla were to redesign the Edison dynamos completely, then he would give Tesla $50,000. When Tesla successfully redesigned the model, Edison pointed out that Tesla did not understand American humor, and instead, offered him a small raise for his hard work. From there, Tesla attempted to introduce new, more efficient electricity models to Edison but Edison completely disagreed with Tesla and did everything he could to sabotage Tesla's success.

Later, Tesla went on to pursue his passion and moved along to a new company with George Westinghouse, the owner of a Pittsburgh electricity company. There, Westinghouse completely funded Tesla's research and offered Tesla a royalty agreement that would secure him profits from future sales based on his successful research. When Tesla proved to be successful, Westinghouse took recognition for Tesla's successes and allowed everyone to believe that it was he who had successfully produced the new form of electricity.

These were not the only two cases where Machiavellianism sabotaged Tesla and his recognition for his hard work. Over the years, many people took patents filed by Tesla and developed their own systems and then took responsibility for everything, including the work that Tesla had contributed to their systems. A famous example is Guglielmo Marconi who was long seen as the "father of radio" despite having gotten his templates from Tesla's breakthrough. In these circumstances, Tesla simply did not have the cunning wit or social intelligence of the others which resulted in him being taken advantage of. It wasn't until recent years, long after Tesla's passing, that people began to realize that the true mastermind behind these developments was none other than Tesla himself.

Manipulators and people who have a deep thirst for power know that the key to power is keeping their own hands clean while allowing others to do the dirty work for them. Manipulators thrive on taking advantage of people who have a genuine passion and interest in their work and their lives by offering them the opportunity to fulfill their passion while the manipulator takes recognition for the work being done. This is how manipulators prove that they are powerful, by keeping themselves out of the work itself and then robbing others of their rightful recognition. Instead, they offer the passionate individual minimal amounts of recognition and tiny rewards for their work as they absorb all of the meaningful recognition being offered by others.

When a manipulator does not feel as though they are getting what they want, they will often use obscene tactics to attempt to manipulate others into doing more so that they can get greater recognition. For example, when Edison made a genuine offer to Tesla in the amount of $50,000, he then laughed it off as a joke when Tesla followed through on his part of the deal. This type of behavior frequently happens from manipulators who are often unwilling to be held accountable for their agreements or offerings but will appear as though they are honest until the point where they get their desires met. As soon as they have what they want, they gaslight the other person into believing that the deal never existed or that it was different than they remember, then they manipulate them into believing that they do not have to pay up their end of the deal. Often, the manipulator will corner the other person into a position where they are unable to back out or take back their offering, leaving them feeling the painful effects of being taken advantage of by someone else.

The best way to protect yourself against being taken advantage of, in favor of someone else receiving your rightful recognition, is by taking pride in your work and taking accountability in your deals. If you agree to do something for someone, always cover your bases and ensure that there are no loopholes that could be used to dupe you out of your rewards. Never let someone else take advantage of you and always make sure that you protect your right to speak up and take responsibility for your own work. If you find yourself being taken advantage of by someone, create the opportunity for you to terminate that connection so that you can surround yourself with people who are not manipulative and cruel. Do not fall for the charm of others, always get things in writing, and protect yourself even if it seems unnecessary. You never know when you may be taken advantage of by others. Remember, a Machiavellian or manipulative person rarely looks like a dangerous person until you are already too deep in their games.

## People Do Things for their Own Reasons, Not Ours

People are driven by their own inner desires, not the desires of those around them. Even in instances where it seems like someone is being driven by someone else's desires, the underlying driving force is actually their personal desires or reasons. For example, say you knew a loved one who smoked, and you wanted them to stop smoking because you were afraid of losing them to cancer. If you were to spend each visit letting them know how dangerous smoking is and asking them to stop because you did not want to lose them, they would likely not quit smoking because this would not be meaningful enough to motivate them. Even though it is a genuine and kind cause, it simply isn't *their* reason. Therefore, they do not personally feel driven by it. However, if this same person was to fall ill and find that smoking was the primary cause of their illness and they wanted to overcome the illness, they may find this to be meaningful enough to cause them to quit smoking. The key difference here is that they are being driven by something that is meaningful to them personally, rather than something that is meaningful to you.

Often, if people try to do things that are meaningful to someone else but not to themselves, they will find themselves struggling to stay committed to such a cause. This is not because they do not care about those around them or the opinions of those around them, but because they are simply not personally motivated enough to completely change their behaviors. The same goes for virtually everyone. People do things for their own reasons, not for our reasons.

Manipulators realize that they need to appeal to people's own self-interest when they are recruiting them in their deceitful games, so they use this knowledge to make it seem like it was the other person's idea and not their own. This is how a manipulator can hide the fact that they have orchestrated the entire thing because they make it seem like the other person came to the conclusion on their own. This type of manipulation is particularly challenging to recognize and overcome because people do not want to admit that they have been manipulated or that they made a personal decision to support someone in a shady agenda. For that reason, most people who are manipulated will not even realize it, and if they do get a feeling that they have been manipulated, they will attempt to justify their situation or hide it to avoid being caught. To admit that they have been manipulated and that their actions contributed to something bad would feel painful, so in many cases, the manipulated individual will hide the manipulation so well that even they cannot see the manipulation. This is not because they are unaware of it but because they have found a way to mentally justify it or cope with it to avoid feeling the immense pain or embarrassment that would come from admitting it.

People in power know that appealing to someone's self-interest allows that person to feel as though they have made the decision themselves, and with that, comes the development of personal reasoning. In other words, with the right manipulation tactics, any person can formulate a reason for why they will do something, even if that something is seemingly uncharacteristic of whom they are. Manipulators or people who engage in things, like Machiavellian power, will take advantage of this knowledge and encourage people to come up with their own reason as to why they are engaging in the said behavior/s.

A Machiavellian leader or a manipulator will appeal to your personal interests by first trying to gain an understanding of what is valuable to you and what you care about in your life. Typically, most people have some fairly standard core values: family, happiness, financial freedom, and health. However, each person will have their own set of unique values, too. A manipulator will expertly identify these values by listening to you speak and paying attention to what you speak most about, especially when you start exhibiting signs of passion or deep interest. Then, they will use these values to manipulate you to formulate your own reasons as to why you should behave in the way that they want you to behave.

For example, say your boss wants you to start contributing more at work, but they are not in the financial position to offer you any more money. Perhaps you have declined the advanced position because you are not interested in doing more work without earning an increased wage. If your boss were a Machiavellian leader and they knew that slowing down or monitoring your health was of value to you, they would likely say something to the effect of, "Too bad. I bet your age could really benefit from doing less physical work and spending more time relaxing in a new office." This would lead to you feeling as though you may need to take the position due to the benefit of being able to sit more and get off of your feet. In reality, you would be doing more work even though the work would be less physical, and it may even result in an increased level of stress. However, the way your boss worded it leads to you feeling as though you have personal reasons as to why you should consider the offer; thus leading to you likely changing your answer to "Yes" instead of standing by your original "No."

The best way that you can avoid having someone manipulating you through your own sense of reason is to make sure that you develop your self-awareness and that you have a strong understanding of what truly matters to you and why. Any time someone presents you with options or a decision, always take your values into account and honestly consider what matters to you and which option will genuinely meet your needs. Always look at the long goal too. Most manipulators will attempt to manipulate you by assuming that you will only consider the immediate gain that you have and that you will fail to honestly consider the long-term consequences that you may face if you do not achieve said gains. By paying attention to what you stand to gain (or lose) in the future, you give yourself the opportunity to genuinely consider all of the pros and cons of every decision and make a choice based on what fulfills your needs rather than what fulfills someone else's.

You can also protect yourself by considering what someone else is saying and honestly considering the nature of why they are saying it. For example, with the above scenario, your boss was not concerned about your health; they wanted you to take the offer, and they were attempting to manipulate you into taking it. The nature of their opinion was not genuine or considerate towards your needs, but instead, was based on their needs and was meant to shape your opinion. Any time you experience something like this happening, think critically about the situation and do more detective work into the offer itself. Chances are that the decision may not be one that is genuinely good for you, but instead, may be offered by the other person in hopes that they will gain something from you, regardless of whether or not you actually want to offer the said thing in the first place.

## People Rarely Change their Minds even though they are Proven Wrong

Another way that manipulators will use your reasoning to their advantage is by getting you on board with their beliefs knowing that you are unlikely to back out once you have said yes. Getting people to change their minds is much harder than getting them to make an initial decision – since most people stand by their initial judgment on something, even if the alternative or negative information is later presented. This is because staying in agreement with their original belief keeps them united with the group that they have now identified themselves as a part of. For example, if you are a Republican but find that your beliefs are better represented by the Democrats, you might continue to support Republicans, even if you realize that they do not represent your best interest because you do not want to lose your "group". Psychology has shown that staying connected to your chosen group actually stimulates the reward pathway in your brain. Likewise, attempting to remove yourself from your chosen group, even with the desire of joining a new group, can actually trigger the same responses that produce withdrawal symptoms. This means that your brain is literally wired to keep you in compliance with your original decision, even if you no longer believe in it the way that you once did. Changing your mind and choosing a new path, group or label to identify yourself with ultimately requires you to be willing to suffer through those painful symptoms so that you can adjust your perspective and pick a new option.

For most people, instead of attempting to withstand the pains of changing their minds, they engage in what is known as cognitive dissonance. Cognitive dissonance occurs when your beliefs are contradictory; thus creating a dissonance between them. For example, if you believe that all rich people are bad, but you also have the belief that you need to be rich to have a good life, you will experience dissonance. Your brain naturally wants to eliminate the dissonance because the dissonance creates chaos and discomfort within your thoughts. You will either remain poor and live a bad life or grow rich and become a bad person, both of which are not desirable, so your brain seeks to overcome this. Your brain copes by creating the smallest changes possible to maintain your belief system and keep it as close to normal as possible. For this reason, it is unlikely that your opinions about your two basic beliefs will change. You will likely continue to think that being rich means you are bad and being poor means you are living a bad life. Instead of completely changing your core beliefs, you are more likely to develop a new belief, such as one that states that being a bad person is not necessarily such a bad thing, or that living a bad life is not as bad as it sounds. These new beliefs are designed to compensate for the dissonance while still keeping you compliant with your original beliefs. Through this subconscious behavior, you can avoid having to completely change your beliefs and opinions so that you can continue thinking the same way you always have while producing the opportunity to feel good about yourself and your decisions.

Manipulative people know that once you have made a decision, you are unlikely to change your mind. Instead, you are likely to produce new beliefs or opinions to support your current stance. This is much like what happens with choosing through emotions and supporting through logic; you will make a decision and then subconsciously seek to cope with your decision by producing supportive facts that allow you to feel good about your beliefs. This means that if a manipulator can get you to say yes or support them in something, even if you later discover that they are a bad person or their motivations were poor, you are unlikely to turn your back on them. The process of changing your mind requires you to admit that your initial beliefs were wrong and that for a period of time you were supporting something that was unproductive or that may have even gone against your core values. Doing so can be emotionally painful and can come with feelings like shame, embarrassment, guilt, and fear. Most people want to avoid those feelings, so they simply stay on board with their initial opinion and never actually change their minds.

A manipulative person will first use this information to their advantage by presenting you with selective information to get you on board with what they need you for. Typically, they will not tell you anything negative about the situation until after you have already agreed to support them or stand by them in their decision. Even then, a true Machiavellian person will only present you with minimal amounts of negative information. You are more likely to be blindsided by the negative parts later on than you are to ever actually hear them from the Machiavellian – unless they are a piece of necessary information.

Knowing that people who use Machiavellian power and manipulators will use your logic and reasoning in this way means that you can protect yourself by holding permission for you to change your mind. If you find that you have been supporting someone and later discover that they are wrong or even bad, do not continue supporting them because you are afraid to admit that you know. Instead, allow yourself to be willing to admit to your mistake and educate yourself on how you can do better going forward. Being open and honest with yourself, and reserving your right to change your mind means that you can hold yourself in a position where should you find yourself supporting a manipulator or a Machiavellian, you can stop and realign with someone or something that actually supports your values.

Another way that you can avoid having this type of manipulation work on you is by recognizing any time you find yourself producing new beliefs or opinions that are used to support your current core beliefs. If you feel that you are working far too hard to support your current beliefs by constantly having to compensate them and justify them, it may be because they are not presently working for you the way that they need to be. Honestly sitting with yourself and addressing your beliefs and how they may be misrepresenting your honest opinion is the best way to make sure that you are not holding onto beliefs that do not accurately represent you. Once you have addressed these misaligned beliefs, you can go on to shift your perspective at the level of the original beliefs; thus allowing you to stay in control over your position to prevent you from blindly and loyally following manipulators down unwanted paths.

## People Make Decisions Based on Emotion and Justify Them with Facts

People are driven by their emotions, not the facts. Although factual information is important to many people, most people will first make a decision based on their emotions and then will search out the necessary factual information to justify their decision. Many people use this information to their advantage when it comes to influencing other people's behaviors, especially in the corporate world. It is not uncommon for salespeople and corporate leaders to tell you exactly what you want to hear first, appealing to your emotions and encouraging you to feel good about making a decision. Then, they will follow up with facts that reinforce those emotions so that you truly stay on board with the decision and feel like it is the right one for you. In most cases, people will do very little when it comes to appealing to factual information unless those facts directly support your emotional decision-making. They know that if they can get you to emotionally agree to what they want or need from you, then you will produce the facts to justify your choice all on your own.

Not everyone will use emotional decision-making against you, but the reality is that this is one of the most well-known and well-taught skills out there when it comes to industries like sales and marketing. For that reason, it is important that you understand how you are vulnerable from this perspective and what you can do to avoid being duped by someone who may be trying to use this vulnerability to take advantage of you.

The behavior of deciding with emotion and justifying with facts is actually a fascinating psychological cycle that works in an incredible manner. It is particularly common in sales, though it can happen in virtually any and every decision that you need to make in your life, such as choosing whom to marry or which friends you want to keep around in your life. The cycle first launches when you experience a subconscious or intuitive pull to decide in a certain direction on something, such as if you go to a store and feel the pull to purchase a certain pair of shoes that you were drawn to. Then, once this intuitive pull arises, your conscious mind will instantly begin searching for rational reasoning for why you should purchase these shoes. Once it has discovered some rational reasons that it can stand behind, the circle is completed: those reasons are used to justify your emotional signal, so you go ahead and complete the purchase.

The reason why this cycle can be so dangerous is that most people do not acknowledge it or become aware of it. In fact, many people, companies, or marketers who are trying to get you to make a decision will actually appeal to your rational thinking mind instead of your emotional thinking mind, attempting to get you to justify your decision rationally. As a result, it is fairly simple to feel like you are in control because, mentally, you are making most of your decisions from your rational mind, allowing you to realize things like, "No, I don't want to spend that money" or "No, I don't really need that" or "No, I'm not really interested in doing that." As soon as they stop appealing to your rational mind, however, it becomes much more challenging for you to remain in control. Manipulative people know this.

Unlike those who attempt to appeal to your rational mind, manipulators will attempt to appeal to your emotional mind. They know how to stimulate specific emotions, or dreams of specific emotions, within your mind so that you begin experiencing that intuitive pull to say yes or comply with what they have offered. This is exactly how many politicians, salespeople, and expert manipulators have appealed to such a large crowd of people and increased their loyal following. They do so by appealing to their target audience's emotions and offering things that make their audience *feel* good. Then, they justify their decisions with facts to help their audience feel as though their decisions make sense. In many cases, those facts are not even complete and, sometimes, they are not even entirely relevant to the topic at hand. However, because they have already gotten their followers agreeing on an emotional level, they can maintain the agreement and support their audience in feeling good about it with small amounts of facts to keep their rational minds quiet.

This type of manipulation is especially common in personal relationships, such as those shared between lovers, friends or relatives. In these relationships, you tend to feel a deep emotional connection to the other person that leaves you continually searching for logical reasons to justify your desire to stay in the relationship, even if it is toxic to you. This is why many people find themselves feeling trapped in toxic or dangerous abusive relationships because their emotions work in favor of the abusive or toxic person and their logic continually seeks to support their decision to stay. Abusive people know this and often use this as a method to manipulate people into staying in relationships with them, even if the other person knows better. This is why even people who are not considered to be particularly vulnerable to abusive relationships can be roped in and victimized by the abuse: because no one is truly completely immune to this form of manipulation.

The best way that you can protect yourself against getting pulled into manipulative tactics through your emotions is by slowing down and critically thinking about anything you are engaging in when your initial interest was based on emotions. Any time you find yourself feeling emotionally charged to make a decision, especially if that decision sounds too good to be true, stop and give yourself a moment to think rationally and search for unbiased facts surrounding the decision that you are seeking to make. Honestly consider whether or not it is going to be a good decision for you and then make the decision based on your rational thinking, even if it feels challenging or uncomfortable. If it feels as though you honestly cannot do this, first seek to find the honest facts and then back up your facts by determining how your emotions will feel long term. For example, say you are afraid to end a toxic relationship because you are afraid that you will be alone and you will never experience happiness again. Realistically, this is untrue, and this is just your emotional mind attempting to control your logical one. By recognizing that you can actually surround yourself with positive people and feel a greater sense of happiness after terminating the toxic relationship (because you will have more energy to contribute to other relationships in your life), this becomes a much easier decision. Always seek to make your decisions in the most unbiased way possible, and be willing to look at the alternatives or the long-term game if you are struggling to make a decision that is truly going to support you in feeling your best.

## People Want To Feel in Control of Their Lives

As a human, you never want to feel as though you have no control over your life or the decisions that you make. For this reason, you will avoid making decisions regarding anything where it feels like the true choice is not in your power. You may have noticed that any time you spent time with another human who was particularly controlling, you felt as though this person was not enjoyable to spend time with and you may have even terminated the relationship. This is because spending time with this person took away from your feeling of control and the experience overall was uncomfortable.

Staying in control feels good because it feels like freedom, and freedom is something that humans crave. We do not like to be restricted by the feelings of pressure or feel we are no longer able to make our own decisions. These types of feelings can provoke fear and discomfort. This is why the entire western world is built on the concept of "freedom". Realistically, we are not free, but we feel as though we are because we have the power to make many of our own life decisions, such as where we will work, where we will live, and whom we will marry.

If we were truly free, we would be able to do anything without experiencing any negative repercussions from our decisions. Naturally, this would have serious consequences. In a truly free society, someone could commit a serious crime and never be held accountable for their actions because they had the freedom to behave in such a way. So, countries with a democracy produce a sensation of freedom by operating on a structure that gives us choices. Through having a society built on choices, we feel as though we are experiencing freedom, but what we are truly experiencing is the opportunity to choose between a controlled series of choices. In other words, our life is built on multiple choice questions where the answers are limited, but they still provide options nonetheless.

Ideally, a society built in such a way should still possess a fairly healthy amount of freedom because people can still make ample decisions about their own lives. Unfortunately, building a society in this way can also lead to many difficulties when only a select few people are in charge of the decisions that we get to make. These limitations and difficulties are not restricted to societies and government either. In fact, controlled decisions are used in many different forms in society. For example, any time you walk into a store and go to purchase something, you have controlled decisions based on the number of items available to you, and while these items do vary, they only vary so much. For example, there may be a select number of colors or a limited number of variations made for each style of clothing that is available for you to purchase. In this circumstance, it feels like you have options, but in reality, the options are controlled or limited. There are only so many choices for you to pick from.

This may seem somewhat manipulative or restrictive, but in many cases, this type of controlled decision practice is not meant to be manipulative. In most circumstances, the limited number of options is based on the fact that it would simply be too challenging to offer every single option. For example, a single clothing store simply cannot offer every single style of clothing in every single color. This would be expensive and unsustainable, so it is not something that clothing companies offer. The same goes for politics: attempting to offer every single possible option would be nearly impossible. Furthermore, offering too many options leaves people struggling to make decisions because there are simply too many things for them to consider, so they become overwhelmed. In a situation where you want people to purchase something or vote on something, having too many options impedes your audience's ability to make a decision and leaves you either struggling to make sales or struggling to come to a solid conclusion. For that reason, controlled decisions are actually a productive solution and can be extremely helpful in most circumstances.

Still, there are many circumstances where people can use controlled decision-making as a way to manipulate other people into making the preferred decision based on the manipulator's preferences. There is a saying that goes, "If you can get the bird to walk into the cage on its own, it will sing much more prettily." In other words, if a manipulator can get you to decide to do something on your own account, not only will you do it but you will also do it well because you feel as though it was your choice that brought you there. Knowing this, manipulators will combine controlled decisions with other tactics, such as playing on your emotions, to get you to decide in their favor. Through this type of behavior, they can honestly say that you are doing only what you agreed to do and that you made such a decision because it was the right decision for you. This logic is challenging to fight because there is rarely a way to truly prove that you were manipulated into believing that this decision was your decision when it truly was not a decision you would have come to on your own. It can also lead to feelings of self-depreciation if you find yourself wondering why and how you bought into the manipulation. Many people who have been manipulated in this way find themselves asking things like "Why can I never make a decent decision?" or "Why am I so stupid?" because the manipulator leads you into believing that there was no manipulation taking place, even when there was. If this happens often enough, your self-esteem and your value in yourself depreciate, and it becomes even easier for them to manipulate you because you no longer trust yourself or your decision-making skills.

In many cases, there is not much that you can do to avoid the repercussions of manipulative controlled decision practices. For example, you cannot force a store to carry more products or force the government to behave in a specific way that is more considerate of the people it is meant to look out for. While these changes can happen, they often take time and persistence. For them to happen, a number of people will need to get on board with the same goals and work together to pressure companies or governments into changing the available options so that the options are favorable. This can help minimize the amount of negative manipulation taking place and optimize the controlled decision-making system to work in favor of those it is meant to serve. Still, even with a large number of people on board, it can take time and consistently applied pressure to get these changes to take place.

The best way that you can avoid being subjected to these types of manipulative behaviors is to recognize them when they are taking place and educate yourself on the options available to you and what rights you have in your position. If you are being exposed to manipulative controlled decisions by someone or something that you can avoid, avoiding that person or place may be your best option to avoid being manipulated. However, if you are being forced to make a decision, make a decision that is going to work in your best interest and then, if it truly means something to you, learn about how you can contribute to making the system better so that your options are more reasonable in the future.

You should also beware of anyone who is trying to pressure you into making decisions by giving you limited options, especially when these limited options do not seem favorable, and the decision is being applied with pressure. For example, say someone is trying to sell you something, and they present you with two offers. As they present you with these two offers, they begin applying a significant amount of pressure and start bombarding you with reasons why one option is better than the other option. It is likely that this type of scenario features manipulation, as this person is trying to pressure you into feeling as though your only options are to purchase one or the other. By bombarding you with information and applying pressure, they are trying to encourage you to forget that saying "no" is also an option. Through this tactic, they can get you to purchase something from them even if you did not need it or even want it in the first place. This type of behavior is manipulative and can lead to you making unwanted decisions because you feel as though you have no control over the situation. To avoid these types of experiences, the best thing you can do for yourself is to remember that "no" is always an option and empower yourself to say "no" when the options being presented to you are not reasonable. This way, you can avoid making an unwanted decision in the face of stress because you will remember how to take back control and make a rational decision that actually fits your needs or desires.

## People Want to Be Part of Something Larger Than Themselves

Humans are driven by their need to be a part of a community. Our longing for love, acceptance, and company keeps us constantly searching for something to be a part of. Most of us do not feel "complete" unless we are a part of something bigger than ourselves, often in alignment with a larger group of other people. This is why many people support things like religions and cultures because these are opportunities to be a part of something that is bigger than just themselves. Together, the community joins to be a part of something meaningful, often engaging in traditions as a way to keep themselves working towards something that has a purpose. Based on this particular need or behavioral law, people are drawn into various groups that are larger than themselves and that align with their core beliefs and values.

The type of power that originally set out to manipulate people based on this human nature was charlatans. Initially, charlatans would focus on building small groups around themselves and then selling them things such as magical elixirs that were promised to grant blessings such as immortality and superior health. One day, they accidentally stumbled on this law of human nature when they began seeing the groups around them grow larger and larger. As they found, the bigger the group became, the more powerful they managed to be. In fact, they would become so powerful that even when people realized that their elixirs were often bogus, their other loyal followers would defend them and protect them against the disbelievers. Any deficiencies in their ideas would be hidden by the sheer mass of their following and the devotion that their "fans" had towards them and their "abilities".

Over many decades, charlatans learned how to refine and perfect the art of building large crowds and would do so over and over again, molding their crowds into loyal followers and turning their loyal followers into a cult. Once the minds of their following were shaped, the charlatan would be able to maintain their power and control and could guarantee that they would lead a prosperous and bountiful life that would be protected by their followers.

As you can see through charlatanism, using this basic human law in the form of manipulation can quickly result in massive amounts of people being swept off their feet and carried away in the current before they even know what is happening to them. In most cases, these well-meaning people have no desire to be a part of a cult, but instead, they are simply following their subconscious need to be a part of something bigger than themselves. They find themselves in cults when they fail to understand the tactics of the charlatan or the cult leader, and often, they have no idea that they are inside of a cult in the first place. This is because they have been successfully manipulated by the leader to believe that they are doing something for the greater good of society and they believe that anyone not doing the same must be dangerous, evil, or simply wrong.

To avoid falling victim to this dangerous form of manipulation, you must understand how charlatanism works and how individuals can use manipulation to lead people to form a cult around them. It is important that you realize that cults do not always look the way that you may picture a cult to look. It is not always about paying money to join the group and blindly following the leader as one person clearly benefits from the ignorance of the rest. Cults can come in all shapes and sizes and do not always follow the same obvious structure that traditional cults do. For example, many famous people and famous brands could be considered cult leaders because they formulate massive followings of people who deeply believe in them and their purpose and who will defend them no matter what. Even when that person or brand does something "bad" or "wrong" their following will find a way to justify it and sweep it under the rug with them so that they do not risk losing their connection to the larger community that they are surrounded by.

The best way to understand how charlatanism and cults work is to understand how cults are built. This is not so that you can go on to develop your own cult, but instead, so that you can understand the methodology behind them so that you can avoid being drawn into one and build immunity to the manipulation tactics that they use. By having a deep understanding of the five steps used to build a cult, you can educate yourself on what these steps look like and avoid being duped by them yourself.

The first step that goes into building a cult is attracting attention and building the interest of people who may be willing to join your cult. Most people will do this, not through clear actions, but instead, through deceptive words that do not fully explain everything that you need to know. Typically, they will try and keep the amount of information that you are being offered slim and what they do say will be hazy so that it sounds like they are brilliant but, in reality, they are not sharing anything revolutionary or different. Instead, they are simply using manipulation to inspire your interest and have you curious about what it is that they are doing and why it seems to be working so well for them. Often, what they do share will be more focused on the results and particularly the feelings and visions of a colorful fantasy that they know other people want to experience. They know that as you become more emotionally invested, you will see what you want to see and, as you now know, you will draw the logical conclusions on your own to cement in your support and keep you interested. The best way to avoid being manipulated by this type of action is to ask for very specific details and see how a charlatan responds. If they are attempting to manipulate you, they will struggle to produce any meaningful or direct responses to your questions, proving that you are in fact being duped by them and their vague ways. Always make sure that you question everything and be very critical about the clarity of the responses that you are being offered. If something is not adding up for you, do not try to make sense of it, but instead, move on and realize that there probably is no logical sense to be made since the entire offer is built on manipulation.

Once a charlatan has drawn you in with interest based on vague information, they will always use the process of selling to you through visual and sensual descriptions over intellectual ones. This is because a charlatan does not want you to become bored or have you to start thinking critically. You will realize that there are likely many flaws with their offer. For that reason, if you find that a person is consistently sharing dreamy images and elegantly worded fantasies with you but never actually gets into the "why" or "how" of the matter, be cautious. The chances are, the reasoning is all vivid and the benefits that you stand to gain are slim – if there even are any.

Another tactic that some charlatans will attempt to use to produce their desired results is borrowing forms of organized religion or other organized groups to mask their actual power. For example, in some religious cults, the leader will not refer to themselves as a dictator, even if they are leading the group through a dictatorship style of leadership. Instead, they refer to themselves as "priests", "gurus", "shamans" or any other words that they can use to cover up what it is that they are actually trying to do. It is important that you understand that not all people who identify by these labels are actually attempting to manipulate you: many who claim that they identify with such labels genuinely do. However, if you find someone using such a label while also identifying with other qualities of a charlatan, be careful. The chances are that they may be trying to manipulate you.

Step four, when it comes to building a cult following like a charlatan, is masking your true source of income and making it seem as though you are abundantly wealthy through random blessings and not through taking money directly from your followers. If you see someone is surrounding themselves with luxury and flashing off signs of their wealth without ever clearly explaining where their wealth comes from, or by claiming it comes from a flimsy source like low-quality products that you have never heard of, beware. The chances are that their money comes from scamming people and taking money directly from their followers and that it actually has nothing to do with their proposed structure. If you cannot have someone clearly show you where their wealth comes from and how it is produced, they are probably attempting to use the flashy methods of charlatanism to cover up the fact that their wealth comes from their followers.

Finally, a charlatan will always try to produce an "us versus them" system within their groups that always leave their group seeming at odds with the rest of the world. If a manipulative charlatan is duping you, you will know it because they will always attempt to subliminally twist the dynamic of their following to encourage a divide between their cult and everyone else in the world. Through this dynamic, the charlatan knows that they will be faithfully protected by the fact that a human will not change their mind because they do not want to lose their group. So, they will fiercely protect the charlatan to protect their position and stay closely linked with the group that they have grown to identify themselves as a part of, even if it makes no logical or rational sense to anyone, not even themselves.

## People Want to Know Why They Should Do Something Rather Than How

In our society, the word "because" is a powerful word that can encourage almost anyone to do almost anything. This is because the word "because" answers the one question that everyone has: "Why?" People are deeply driven by understanding the reasons why they should do something, not by how it is done. Most humans will not care how they are being asked to do something as long as they understand why they are being asked, even if the reason why is not necessarily meaningful or purposeful. Psychologists theorize that this stems from our childhood and from the conditioning that we receive from our parents when they use statements like "Because I said so." For example, if your parent asked you to do your homework before you played outside and you said, "Why?" your parent would likely answer with something like, "Because I said so" or "Because I told you to." The theory is that we became so used to realizing that "because" meant that there was no other solution that we no longer pay too much attention to what follows the word "because".

We have been conditioned to realize that "because" means it is important and that we probably have no other option. This is not because there truly is no other option, but simply because we have been conditioned to believe that there is not one, or that the other option is not worth considering because it may bring about unwanted consequences. Based on all of this, most people will not actually pay attention to what is said after the word "because" because they have been conditioned to believe that they do not need to. The word itself implies that it is important and that it needs to be done. This was proven by a psychologist who wanted to test to see if this theory held up. They did so by sending a person into an office where there was a lineup of people waiting to use the copying machine. On the first day, the person they sent in asked the line, "Can I use the machine? I need to make copies." On that day, 60% of people said yes, even though they were all waiting in line to do the very same thing. The next day, they sent another person in, and this person asked, "Can I use the machine because I'm in a rush?" On that day, 94% of people agreed to let that person go to the front of the line, even though everyone else was waiting to do the same thing. On the final day, they sent another person in, and this person asked, "Can I use the machine because I need to make five copies?" and on this day, 93% of the line agreed to let that person go first, despite the fact that the reasoning was fairly irrelevant and lacked meaning.

What the psychologist proved was that people were 30% more likely to agree to something simply because someone used the word "because" to provide meaning to their request, even if the meaning was bogus or weak. In most cases, this form of human conditioning and behavior does not amount to much in your day-to-day life. The majority of the things that you hear and agree to are not going to have any form of negative impact on you. Also, most people are unlikely even to be aware of this behavior; thus it is highly unlikely that they are using the word "because" to attempt to manipulate you into doing something that you do not want to do.

The one time that the word "because" will lose its impact on people is if the reasoning is longer. If the reasoning is more than a short sentence long, the person listening is less likely to be duped because they have to start listening again to hear what is actually going on. For example, if someone says, "This hair conditioner is the best because it has salts from the Dead Sea in it," you are likely to comply with whatever they are requesting, such as by purchasing the hair conditioner. However, if they say, "This hair conditioner is the best because it has salts from the Dead Sea in it, which are meant to exfoliate your scalp and add body to your hair so that you can combat flat hair and dandruff," they have carried on too long. At this point, you will have tuned back in and begun listening again, meaning that your rational mind is also tuning in and formulating an opinion about what they have said. The chances are that the opinion will help you to realize that paying $55 for a bottle of off-brand conditioner that is made with low-quality ingredients is not ideal and that you do not care about the Dead Sea salts in the bottle. Or, if you do care, you may move on and research the benefits and see if there are any better and more reasonably priced brands available for you to purchase. Both of these circumstances do not benefit the seller; therefore, they have failed to gain the manipulative benefits of using the word "because".

While most people are unaware of what the word "because" actually does to your mind, there are still many people that are aware of this conditioning, and will use it to their advantage when it comes to getting people on board with what they are requesting. In fact, this very technique is taught in practices like neurolinguistics programming (NLP) to support practitioners in being able to speak directly to the subconscious mind to produce their desired results. Many people who educate others on sales strategies and marketing strategies will also educate on using the word "because" as a way to inspire people to take the desired action without realizing that they are being manipulated into doing so.

Knowing how to avoid this type of unwanted manipulation ultimately requires you to start paying attention any time you hear someone saying "because" so that you can avoid being manipulated. Make sure that the moment you hear the word "because" you start critically thinking about the words that follow it and you honestly assess whether or not they actually matter. Even if the other person is not trained to realize that this is a form of manipulation, or if they are doing it with a complete lack of awareness around what they are doing, you need to pay close attention. If the words after "because" support a bogus or irrelevant reason, press for more information or attempt to get a more meaningful reason as to why you should actually do the requested actions. If they do not have one, there is probably not one, and they are simply trying to get their way through reason rather than intellect.

# People Want to Be Treated as Unique or Special

People adore being treated like they are special or unique in some way as this makes them feel important and nurtures their sense of ego. Often, this is not intended to be shallow or superficial. Instead, they genuinely feel good when they are being treated like they are important. Feeling important often coincides with receiving positive attention, which is something that every single human, from babies to the elderly, craves. When you receive positive attention, it boosts your self-esteem, improves your self-confidence, and leaves you feeling like you are capable of achieving anything that you desire in life. When someone loves you unconditionally, shows you an immense amount of support, or treats you like your talents are something especially unique, it feels *good*. You start to take pride in what you are doing, and you may even do a little more so that you can show off even more of your talents and receive an even greater amount of positive attention or praise from the people who are stimulating these feelings in you.

When this is done in a healthy manner, seeking and receiving positive attention from others and feeling important is a great thing. However, this type of behavior can also quickly become toxic and leave you heavily vulnerable to manipulation. For example, in abusive relationships, an abuser may verbally lift you up and make you feel special and important so that you feel *really* good, only to withdraw all of the attention for seemingly no reason so that you feel as though you have done something wrong. In these types of relationships, the special attention was given only so that you would become dependent on that one person who made you feel really good about yourself, leaving you extra vulnerable to their manipulative and abusive ways.

This is not only done in abusive relationships between lovers, relatives, or friends either. This type of behavior happens on a regular basis from manipulative people all the time. In many cases, manipulative leaders will use this type of behavior to manipulate their entire audience into feeling important so that they can manipulate their audience into becoming dependent on them and the attention they provide. The same can happen in sales or amongst corporate individuals. People will try to win you over by making you feel important and smart, and then, once they have, they manipulate you into giving them what they want and then completely abandon you once you do.

Amongst manipulative leaders, some of the most common manipulative power plays that play on people's desire to feel special include dumbing themselves down, using selective honesty, and playing the courtier to others. Through these three actions, they can "butter people up" so that they are vulnerable to their other manipulative behaviors; thus leaving the manipulator in the perfect position to get whatever they want. If you want to avoid being manipulated by having someone stroke your ego while they stab you in the back, you need to be on the lookout for these behaviors and practice protecting yourself any time you see them being enacted.

If you see someone dumbing themselves down, it is typically obvious because they often pretend they do not know anything. This is done as a way to try and make you feel like you are superior and have plenty to teach them, so you feel as though you are important and like you have much to offer. When you are in this position, you do not see the manipulator as a threat so you let your guard down and you are no longer on the lookout for manipulative behaviors. If you notice that someone is frequently commenting on how smart you are and acting as though they know very little about things, beware. This is especially true if the situation does not seem to add up, such as if a person pretends they know less about their own profession than you do. Unless they are brand new to the profession or they truly do not care about it, the chances are they already know, and they are simply letting you pretend like you are outsmarting them so that you feel important and wise. You may be tempted to see this as a lack of confidence or low self-esteem, and in some cases, this may be true. However, the more likely reason is that the person is attempting to manipulate you and wants you to stop seeing them as a threat so that you are perfectly positioned for their manipulative antics.

You also need to be cautious any time you hear someone holding back information and attempting to keep things vague or very specific. When it comes to this form of manipulation, the manipulator often knows that you are going to be on the lookout for vagueness and misinformation. For that reason, they will likely be very specific but only about certain things. They may attempt to skirt around certain problems or control the conversation by giving a great amount of detail about something that is only partially relevant to the actual situation at hand. In these circumstances, withholding the truth is rarely a result of the person not being knowledgeable. Instead, it is more likely that they know that you do not want to hear everything they have to say, so they only tell you the parts that they believe will interest you.

Lastly, if you see someone trying to play the courtier to you, be cautious. Playing the courtier means that they are attempting to walk the balance between pleasing you, but not pleasing you too much. Through this, a courtier will always be very cautious about how much they tell you and how much they talk about themselves. Typically, they will try and get you to talk about yourself more and will show great interest in you, often only sharing enough about themselves to make the conversation seem balanced. After all, exclusively talking about you or asking about you would make it obvious that they were up to something, and exclusively talking about themselves would draw attention to themselves. A courtier seeks to bring balance by very carefully speaking about themselves and asking about you, always attempting to draw a balance between how much they share and how it looks to you. They want to praise you and build you up, but they do not want to do it to the point that it seems like they are trying to suck up to you or butter you up for something. By balancing the conversation out by building you up slowly and consistently, they seem to "blend in" and stay under your radar. By blending in this way, however, a courtier takes true control because they can collect information from you while not giving you very much in return. This means that they can uncover everything they need to know to manipulate you while also completely covering their tracks by having you let your guard down around them. In this way, the courtier comes in completely unsuspectingly, takes control, and can do virtually anything they desire without anyone ever realizing that they were manipulating them.

# Chapter 3: The Six Scientific Principles of Persuasion

The topic of persuasion has been researched for more than 60 years as scientists seek to uncover what exactly influences a person to say "yes" to something. The results that have risen from these scientific studies are rather surprising and have taught many people how they can influence others to say "yes" when they are asking for a specific request to be approved. From the position of the person who is not making the decision, it may seem easy to assume that one would weigh all of the pros and cons of their decision before landing on their final answer. However, science has shown that there are actually some very basic things that play into how a person will decide to say either "yes" or "no" based on a few basic shortcuts. These shortcuts exist because we live in a world where there is a constant pile of information being dropped into our laps, and if we were to attempt to weigh out the pros and cons of every decision fully, we would never have time to decide anything. We would be overloaded with decisions to make and things to consider, and it would result in some serious setbacks, ultimately rendering this more rational-based decision-making style useless.

According to science, there are six scientific principles of persuasion. These are the only principles responsible for how people make decisions based on what we currently know. These principles have been scientifically proven by Robert B. Cinaldini, psychology professor and author, in his book *Influence*. We are going to explore what these six principles are and how you can become consciously aware of them so that you can always stay in conscious control of your decision-making skills. Again, while most people will have no idea that these factors even come into play when you are making a decision, a select few people who dabble in Machiavellian practices will attempt to use these principles against you. Staying clearly aware of them will ensure that you are always consciously making decisions in your favor and that genuinely serve your highest good without being unknowingly manipulated by another person.

## Reciprocity

The first principle that encourages people to say "yes" when they have been asked a question is reciprocity. If you have given someone something, they feel obliged to say yes to give you something back because they feel as though they owe you in one way or another. This is true even if you have offered them the said thing as a gift or without the intention of receiving anything back from them. The same goes in the opposite direction too. Any time someone gives you something or does something nice for you, you feel obligated to do something to reciprocate the said action.

A great way to understand how reciprocity works is to consider a study that was conducted in restaurants between waitstaff and their clients. This study proved that any time a waiter or waitress brings you some form of a gift along with the receipt, you are more likely to leave them a larger tip in exchange for the gift. While most people would believe that such a small act does not influence behavior at all, the reality is that it does. The study proved that a single mint offered at checkout increased tips by 3%, but when two mints were offered, the tips increased by 14%. If the waiter or waitress was obvious about the offering of the mints, such as by offering one mint before leaving the table, then turning back and saying something like, "For you fine people, here's an extra mint!" the tip was increased by 23%.

Manipulative people can take advantage of this type of behavior by ensuring that it is obvious any time they offer you something or do something nice for you. In making it obvious or pointing it out, they know that you will feel subconsciously obligated to say "yes" when it comes time to return a favor for them, which they most definitely plan on cashing in on. Typically, they already know what they want from you before they even offer you the nice gift or act of kindness, making the entire thing a manipulative sham.

## Scarcity

One big way that people can be manipulated through scarcity is something that high-quality brands use to secure higher sales numbers. People like to have something that is unique and that no one else has, so when they know something is scarce, they are more likely to want to have it. Manipulative people have been using this information to their knowledge for years, knowing that people want what others can't have. This is tied directly with the human behavior of feeling special and unique.

A great example of this in business is with Birken Bags. Birken Bags are a high-quality bag that cost tens of thousands of dollars to purchase because they are a fashion icon that represents power and status. You might wonder what makes a Birken bag so special and why anyone would be willing to pay tens of thousands of dollars for a purse, and the reasoning is simple. Only a few hundred bags are made every single year, and you have to be on a waiting list or a special list to purchase the bag. That's right, it's not a first-come-first-serve system, but instead, it is a most-loyal-best-served system with Birken. By making their bags scarce and making the purchasing process meaningful and special, this company can profit on the human desire to feel special and unique.

# Authority

People want to be a part of something bigger than themselves, which means that they need to follow some form of leader or authoritative figure that guides them through the process of being a part of that "something bigger". One big way that manipulative people will manipulate others is through creating a sense of authority and leading people from that authoritative position. This is why people in the business world will lead with their credentials over any other information, to establish a position of authority and immediately get others paying attention to them and subconsciously wanting to follow their directions.

For example, a study was done in a real estate company where realtors were able to increase their appointment bookings by 20% and their signed contracts by 15% simply by introducing their agents as authoritative figures. Instead of saying, "Sandra is going to help you today," for example, they would say, "Meet Sandra, she is the head of our sales and has over 20 years' experience in selling homes." This simple change leads to a fairly healthy impact on their sales, proving that a simple persuasive technique could have a significant impact on a company's bottom line. The same goes for virtually anyone, though, as this persuasive principle is not restricted to sales. Any time someone establishes themselves as an expert, whether it be in a self-help industry, as a religious leader, or even simply in your group of friends, that person will always receive more promising results from their requests than anyone else.

# Consistency

People require consistency when it comes to persuading them to say "yes" to something. When someone is exposed to something consistently, they are more likely to be interested in it and saying yes becomes easier as they feel familiar with the offer that they are receiving. For example, they say that the average person has to see a piece of marketing about the same company seven times before they recognize it, and up to or beyond 14 times before they are actually willing to look into it and make a decision. That is unless the company themselves approaches the individual first and creates the connection. In that case, other persuasive measures can be involved to quicken the process and increase the person's likelihood of saying "yes."

When people are seeking to influence someone into agreeing with them, they will always seek to expose them to the idea several times over before they actually ask for the said person to take advantage of the offer. Through this behavior, they increase their chances of receiving a positive response and making the sale, closing the deal or getting the favor they wanted.

# Liking

If someone does not like someone or something, they will almost definitely say "no" the minute they are asked to make a decision regarding that person or thing. People do not like being involved with people or things that they do not like. It is as simple as that. So, when someone tries to persuade someone into saying "yes" or agreeing upon something, they will almost always do so by first gaining the admiration and appreciation of the person. For example, a company will first seek to gain your admiration before attempting to sell to you because this way they know that you are more likely to do so.

An example of how effective the simple basis of liking someone or something is can be shown by a study that was done between MBA students in two well-known business schools. In this study, one group of students entered negotiations with the rule that "time is money; get straight to business" whereas the other group entered negotiations on the premises of "exchanging personal information prior to negotiations to identify a similarity before you begin". In the group that valued time and money over personal connections, only 55% of the negotiations reached an agreement. In the group that valued personal connection first, 90% of the negotiations ended in a successful outcome that was agreed upon by both parties. The outcomes that were reached by those who had established personal connections were also calculated to be 18% more valuable to both parties than those reached by the ones who were more focused on their exchange of time and money. If people are truly looking to persuade you into getting on their side and working in their favor, they are likely going to do so by starting on a personal connection and then working up from there.

## Consensus

People will always look for a common consensus between others when they are uncertain about what decision they should make. By looking at the actions and behaviors of other people, they can determine whether or not they want to do something or engage in something based on what other people are doing and the results that they are experiencing. This is actually how peer to peer sales and social marketing work, by using the positive testimonies and the marketing offered by existing clients to encourage new clients to begin purchasing from them too.

A great example of this can be seen in the growing trend in social marketing strategies. For example, in the past ten years, being an "influencer" on social media has become a serious career path that can offer serious income to anyone who engages in this strategy. Essentially, those who are becoming influencers are simply marketing for other companies and being paid to do so. However, they are successful in doing so because they generate a large following that trusts in them and believes in their opinions. Through this trust, they can leverage their name and increase the number of sales companies earn, which increases even further as their following goes ahead and purchases the endorsed product and agrees that it is, in fact, a great product. Through this domino-effect marketing strategy, companies can increase their sales infinitely while also maximizing their brand awareness through social media with significantly less time and money invested in the marketing process.

# Chapter 4: Clever Mind Control Techniques

One aspect of dark psychology lies in mind control and people's desire to control how others think, behave, and decide upon things. Using the right mind control techniques, people can essentially move past your conscious mind and into your subconscious mind to encourage you to behave in a certain way without you ever realizing what they are actually doing. A common example of a practice that emphasizes mind control techniques is NLP, where practitioners are trained to speak to the subconscious mind of people using psychologically-backed practices. In a positive environment, NLP practitioners can use this psychological practice to help people overcome fears, addictions, and certain unwanted behavioral patterns through the act of spoken word. In dark psychology, however, practices like NLP are used as a way to activate mind control and unknowingly pressure people into doing things that they likely wouldn't do otherwise, such as make a certain purchase or engage in a particular behavioral pattern. In this chapter, we are going to explore nine clever mind control techniques that people using dark psychology could potentially use against you if you weren't already aware of what to look out for to avoid such manipulation.

## Flooding Smile

One way that people who want to practice mind control can embrace the behavioral law of people wanting to feel special is with the flooding smile. This simple technique can be used to make people feel as though they are unique and that they are special from others, and it truly takes no time at all. For it to be achieved, you simply delay your smile when you are meeting someone for the first time. Instead of smiling right away and leading them to feel like you smile at everyone, delay the smile by a few seconds. Then, smile first with your lips and let the smile move through to your eyes and wash over your whole face. This slow smiling strategy helps people feel like they are special by making it seem like you don't smile at just anyone; thus causing them to start liking you more immediately.

## Make Anyone like You

A crafty tool that persuasive people use allows them to make anyone subconsciously like them far more. It works very simply: you increase the amount of attention that you offer to one single person to show that they are more special than anyone else that you are spending time with. The key is to avoid doing it in a creepy or uncomfortable way, so people who are using this as a manipulative strategy will casually increase their attention on the person they are interested in while also trying to make a fairly even balance between others. By giving someone slightly more attention and making that attention slightly more meaningful than the attention begin given to anyone else, you cause their subconscious mind to recognize this attention and instinctively start liking you right away. This is best used in a group of three or more people so that you can really highlight that the attention being given to someone else is more or better quality than the attention being given to others.

## Repeat Yourself

When you want someone to agree with you, you need to repeat yourself to start persuading their mind to believe in the same way that you believe. For someone who is trying to be manipulative, the best way to do this is to avoid complaining while increasing the amount of interest that they show in the desired topic. For example, say you want your group of friends to do something together, but your friends think that the said activity is boring or uninteresting. Instead of complaining and begging them to go with you, you could begin casually talking about how awesome the activity is and how it is clearly superior to any other activity. Studies have shown that acting in this way can improve people's interest by up to 90% after just three times of repeating how awesome the said activity is. This means that your friends would be more likely to agree to go with you than they would be if you were to ask, have them say no, and then you complain and beg them to join you.

## Synchronized Activities

Performing synchronized activities is said to increase the amount of connection between two people, according to scientific studies. If you want someone to like you more or show greater interest in you, all you need to do is ask them to engage in a synchronized activity with you. This will increase the amount of connection they feel with you which will make them instinctively like you far more than almost any other activity that you could attempt to practice together. Some great synchronized activities that can be used for this include walking, singing, biking or attending a class where you are both being taught the same things, such as painting or cooking.

## Be Quiet

For people who want to be heard more or have their opinion considered, the best way to do so is to give the other person control over the conversation – at least at first. You want to begin the conversation by allowing the other person to talk, and asking questions that encourage them to share more. Once they are done sharing, they will eventually ask for your opinion. After they do, they will feel obligated to listen and offer you the same level of attention and consideration based on the principle of reciprocity. This is a clever way that manipulators can ensure that you listen and consider their opinion, even if their opinion seems off, wrong or misguided.

## Ransberger Pivot

Anyone who is looking to win an argument without having a massive blow out and causing the other person to feel threatened can do so using the Ransberger pivot. The Ransberger pivot works by allowing someone else to make their point first as you sit quietly and listen to what they are saying. As you listen, you want to get a deep understanding of their point of view so that you can understand what they care about, what their interests are, and what they are attempting to achieve through their argument. Once they are done, you simply need to create a solution that combines their interests and desires with yours and offer it to them. In doing so, the other person feels as though they are being considered and are getting what they want, and you are also getting what you want, meaning that you both win from this interaction.

## Tell a Lie

Although this is not necessarily a method for manipulation, it is a great way to get out of something that you do not want to do. The key to really getting a lie to work without being questioned is to make the lie slightly embarrassing about yourself. In doing so, people feel uncomfortable and are unlikely to want to press for more information or put any more consideration into what you have said; thus allowing you to successfully bury your lie without ever getting caught. Manipulative people will use this tactic often as a way to avoid getting caught by other people. It works simply by saying something like, "I'm sorry. I can't make it to your dinner party because my IBS has been flaring up lately." This simple small lie will stop the other person from pressuring you to come and will also leave them feeling as though you have not declined simply because you were uninterested or didn't like them. Instead, they will genuinely believe that you couldn't, so they don't like you any less, and you haven't hurt anyone's feelings.

## Control the Conversation

A common manipulation technique that people use is a strategy that allows them to control any conversation in a subtle yet effective manner. The person simply sparks up a conversation with another person and then chooses a specific word that the other person is saying as their "anchor". Then, any time their conversational partner says that word, they nod, smile, or offer some form of positive affirmation every time the word is said. Subconsciously, the person they are talking to will recognize this positive affirmation and will attempt to please the manipulator by using the word repeatedly. This can be used to their advantage if they anchor a word that relates to a request or favor that the manipulator plans on asking the other person at some point during the conversation.

## Perfect Nod

One clever way that manipulators will attempt to manipulate is through nodding. When you nod at a person as you are talking, this creates a natural positive association between you and the other person. What ends up happening is that you show that you are in agreement with the other person and they feel more compelled to agree with you too. You can use this to your advantage by casually and subtly nodding throughout the duration of the conversation before you ever plan on asking for something from someone. Then, when you ask for something from the said person, incorporate a subtle nod into your request. The chances are that they won't even notice that you have done it, but they will subconsciously feel more compelled to agree with you because of the positive agreement that already exists between the two of you.

## The Eyes

A common manipulative practice was scientifically proven as effective during a 1989 study where researchers had two strangers gaze into each other's eyes for two minutes. After the two minutes were up, subjects reported having passionate feelings for the other person. When they looked at the biology of these subjects, they realized that after these tests, subjects had an increase in the neurotransmitters dopamine and oxytocin, the two chemicals responsible for creating the feeling of "love" in people. This can be used to your advantage by simply increasing the amount of casual and positive eye contact that you maintain with people. By increasing the eye contact that you have towards a person that you are interested in, you can cause them to experience the same release of dopamine and oxytocin; thus creating a natural response of love and passion.

# Chapter 5: Techniques from the Best Negotiators

Negotiation is a tool that is used to help two or more people meet under a set of common terms, allowing both or all parties to have their considerations accommodated for within the finalized deal. Negotiating is a common Machiavellian tool used to lure people into believing that they are getting what they want when, in reality, the Machiavellian is the only one truly benefiting from the terms of the final agreement. When it comes to finalizing agreements, Machiavellians have a sneaky way of making sure that every single one of their desired terms is met and they do not care what it costs to get them met. In many cases, a Machiavellian negotiator will leave you with next to nothing, and they will do it in a way that makes it feel as though you were actually accounted for and considered in the process. In reality, they did not care what you gained or lost. They only cared that their needs were met.

In this chapter, we are going to explore nine tactics that manipulative negotiators will use to attempt to get everything they desire from a negotiation, leaving you with absolutely nothing. These tactics are based on the principles of persuasion and the human behavioral laws that you have learned previously in this book.

## We Are Not Driven By Reason

As you know, we are not driven by reason or logic, but instead, by emotions and instinctive "hunches" that we get when we are in certain situations. Manipulative people know this, and they will use your emotions as a way to attempt to get you to understand their logic and side with them, especially when it comes to negotiating. Instead of attempting to overcome your emotions and bring you into a state of rational thinking, a manipulative person will include your emotions as a part of their central strategies. They will appeal to your emotions by connecting on a personal level, creating a sense of comradery, and speaking in a way that validates your feelings and needs from an emotional perspective.

As they continue to negotiate with you, a manipulative person will do everything they can to make you *feel* as though you are in a safe and compassionate environment where you are being considered and accounted for. However, they are only doing this with the intention of bringing down your guard and making you as vulnerable as possible so that when it comes time to offer the final deal, you are far more likely to agree to their terms. When they offer the deal, a manipulative person will continue to make it sound like the deal is working in your favor and like it is something positive for you as well. In reality, while you may have a few small things to celebrate, the chances are that everything you came looking for in the negotiation was completely overlooked and you fell for it simply because you felt good about what was being said. By the time you realize that your negotiation did not work out in your favor, the contracts will have been signed, or the deal will have been issued, and it will be too late for you to back out or make any changes.

**Be a Mirror to Others**

Mirroring people is one of the best forms of flattery, which is why when it comes to things like persuasion, using synchronized activities or mirroring is one of the best ways to get someone to behave in favor of your needs and desires. A great negotiator that is using manipulation to get their way will predict what surprises may arise along the way in the negotiation and draw them in on purpose. Instead of approaching a negotiation ready to argue and win, a great negotiator will approach a negotiation with the ability to focus and listen to everyone around them completely; thus making everyone feel heard, validated, and *good*. From this position, they can also identify anything that may arise that can be used in their favor when it comes to issuing a deal that they know everyone will be on board with.

Instead of trying to rush the process along and get into the deal itself, a manipulative negotiator will slow the process down completely and engage in each step, from listening to thinking the deal through. Through slowing the deal down, they put themselves in control and create the appearance of authority and credibility, causing everyone else in the deal to slow down to their pace and operate on their level. This results in the manipulative person having all of the power; thus leading to everyone else automatically being more likely to agree with them and move forward with anything they have said or offered. In the end, this person is more likely to gain their preferences over anyone else in the negotiation.

# Don't Feel Someone's Pain, Label It

As you read above, a great negotiator will always seek to include emotions as a part of the strategy rather than separate them from the deal altogether. Great negotiators that always seal the deal in their favor know that emotions are inevitable and that they are a major driving force behind people's decision-making, so they use them to their advantage, especially when it comes to pain points. Instead of getting wound up and frustrated when people's pain points are triggered or attempting to separate them from the negotiation entirely, a great negotiator will recognize these pain points and label them. Through showing intentional empathy to those around them, the great negotiator gains the emotional trust of everyone they are negotiating with, therefore, increasing their likeability and making it easier for them to persuade others into agreeing with them.

The key identifying factor with this particular tactic is that the manipulative negotiator will always seek to separate themselves from the label. So, instead of saying, "I recognize your frustration..." they will say, "It seems like you have frustration..." because this takes away from the idea that they have any special interest in the pain of the person they are communicating with. Still, the statement itself shows a sense of empathy and earns other's trust in a way that leaves them feeling as though they are experiencing compassion from the other person, when in reality, they are simply having their emotions used against them in favor of the negotiation.

**Master the Art of "No"**

Manipulative negotiators know that the word "yes" is often meaningless – since it tends to hide the deeper objectives of the person that they are negotiating with. However, when the word "no" arises, this provides an opportunity for both parties to clarify their intentions and needs and move forward with the negotiation, and for that reason, a manipulative negotiator will always make it seem like it is safe for you to say "no" to their terms or ideas. By creating this safe space for you to say "no", a manipulative negotiator knows that not only will you further clarify yourself but you will also be far more likely to listen to them and look at things from their perspective, based on the principle of reciprocity.

By encouraging you to say "no" rather than encouraging you to say "yes", a manipulative person can gain deeper insight into what matters to you and what it is that you truly care about in the exchange of your negotiations. Then, they can use this to further increase your emotional trust in them, making it even easier for them to persuade you into agreeing with them and taking their deal. While it is never guaranteed that hearing "no" makes it easier to get to yes, mastering this tactic is far more effective than banking on a "yes" and finding that it gets switched later on because deeper (and potentially useful) information was not fully revealed.

## Use the Words "You're Right"

A psychologist named Carl Rogers proposed that a therapist can only support a client with real change if they accept the person as who they truly are, also known as using unconditional positive regard. To use positive regard to your advantage, you need to get the other person to say things like, "That's right." This is what manipulative negotiators do when they are attempting to get you to agree with them and change your opinion from where it currently stands. By speaking in a way that has you responding with statements like, "That's right," a great negotiator knows that you are more likely to agree with them and commit to their terms without putting up much of a struggle or requesting many differences on your own behalf. As a result, they win.

It is important to note that a negotiator will always attempt to get you to say, "That's right" and not "You're right." This is because any time a person says, "You're right," they have not personally embraced the information and owned it as their truth. Instead, they have simply stated their agreement. When a person says, "That's right," they are personally embracing the information and accepting it as truth, making them far more agreeable when it comes to closing the negotiation.

## Bend Someone's Reality

A manipulative negotiator will never give more than they were willing to give in the first place, no matter what they may make you think. Despite how they word their sentences and speak their technicalities, a great negotiator will never give you more than they intended to give you in the first place. Instead, they use the negotiation as a way to make it look like everyone is winning, when in reality, they are the only ones coming out with exactly what they expected or wanted. A manipulative negotiator will never split the difference, even if they make it seem as though they have.

The best way to protect yourself against having your reality bent by a negotiator is to avoid believing in the deadlines that they set on their deal. No deal truly ends when the deadline passes as deadlines in negotiations rarely have the detrimental consequences that we are led to believe that they do. If you equip yourself with the knowledge that "no deal is better than a bad deal", then you equip yourself with the patience that you require to get exactly what you were looking for from the other person.

## Create an Illusion of Control

A manipulative negotiator will always attempt to make it look as though they are the ones in control over the situation, even though the truth is that you are both equally in control – since if either of you were to back out, the negotiation would be terminated. When you create the illusion that the other person is in control and then plant seeds for what they want along the way, you make it appear as though they are the ones who created the solution, when in reality, it was the solution you wanted all along. As a result, they are far more likely to agree to your terms based on what you wanted without even realizing that this is what you were going for all along. This is how a Machiavellian negotiator will manipulate anyone into offering them the deal they originally sought while making it look like it was the other person who was in control.

The way that a manipulator will get the negotiation working in their direction is through calibrated questions. Calibrated questions are questions that are asked with the specific intention of manipulating the other person into answering with the desired answer of who asked the question. These calibrated questions require a great deal of emotional self-control so that they do not come across as manipulative or pressured. They also avoid using words that promote the ability for the other person to answer the question with a simple "yes" or "no", and instead, seek to press the other person into producing a more in-depth answer. This persuades the other person to answer in accordance with what they originally wanted, but without making it seem as though they had anything to do with the conclusive answer.

## Guarantee Execution

A great negotiator does not just want to reach a deal, but instead, wants to reach a deal that can be implemented and acted upon. For that reason, they will always seek to generate deals that guarantee execution within a certain time frame. They do this by using a simple question: "How?" For example, "How will we know that we are on track?" or "How will we address the situation if we find out we are off track?" These types of questions encourage the other person to produce a guaranteed, complete answer that can be recorded and saved as something to be acted upon at a later date. Typically, a manipulative negotiator will continue asking how questions until they receive an answer that includes the words "that's right". This way, they know that they are the ones in control over the negotiation and that the other person simply believes that they are in control.

## Drive a Hard Bargain

In people who are not used to negotiating, the process of bargaining produces a great deal of anxiety and unfocused aggression. When it comes time to begin bargaining on what each person will get, people who are unfamiliar with effective negotiating techniques will get uncomfortable and will attempt to force the situation into their favor without much consideration. Instead of using tactful techniques that actually turn the deal in their favor, they will find themselves pressing far too hard to get what they want and showing clear signs of joy and pride when they get small pieces of success thrown their way. This is how a manipulative negotiator knows that they are negotiating with someone who truly has no idea what it takes to achieve their desired results, making their job even easier.

A powerful negotiator will always drive a hard bargain to produce more anxiety in the person with whom they are negotiating with. Then, they will begin stimulating "good feelings" in the other person by mirroring them and making them feel as though their needs and desires are being accounted for. Once the other person is effectively emotionally working in their favor by proving their vulnerability through anxiety and proving their agreeability through pride or joy, the manipulative negotiator will strike with their tough deal. Because they have built the entire deal up based on the principles of persuasion, they know that they will successfully close the deal in their favor with minimal effort or disruption.

# Chapter 6: 19 Predatory Manipulation Techniques

Sociopaths, psychopaths, and narcissists are well-known for using manipulative techniques as a way to exert control over their victims and have their needs or desires met from any interaction. While everyone uses manipulation to one degree or another, these individuals are known for using an excessive amount of manipulation that can often have very serious consequences for all parties involved, but especially their victims. That is what makes these particular manipulators "predators". Predators have 19 techniques that they frequently rely on when it comes to manipulating others and getting what they need from those around them. Almost no one is immune to being targeted by a predator, though people who are already emotionally vulnerable with a low sense of self-esteem or self-confidence are most at-risk. In this chapter, you are going to learn about what these 19 techniques are and how you can protect yourself against them; thus helping you lower your risk of being targeted by a sociopathic, psychopathic, or narcissistic predator.

## Lying

Predators are known for being chronic liars who virtually never tell the truth about anything in their lives. When a predator or manipulator is lying to you, they are attempting to pull you into their web of confusion and chaos where only they truly know what is going on, and even then, they often find themselves forgetting about the lies they have told because there are so many. Predators have zero remorse when they lie. Lying comes easy for them and often, and they become so used to it that they don't even have to think twice about creating a lie. They become so good at it that their lies sound easy to believe because there is no hint that it is a lie in their tone of voice or emotion. To them, it is completely the truth at that very moment.

By creating a chaotic web of lies around you, predators can increase your confusion and keep you vulnerable to them by disillusioning you and bending the reality of the world around you. Since you unknowingly believe their lies, you find yourself having complete faith in everything they have said to you. Once you attempt to use one of their lies to validate something, justify something or hold them accountable for the truth, they will completely spin the lie so that they can keep you feeling confused. Through this, you constantly feel as though you are wrong and they are right, ultimately leading to you no longer relying on your memory or your own perception of reality because it seems as though it is constantly wrong.

Many times, a victim will not realize that they are being lied to by a predator until it has happened so many times that it is hard to deny. At that point, however, other tactics of manipulation and mind control have come into play, leaving the victim feeling completely helpless and as though there is nowhere for them to turn and nothing for them to turn to that can save them from the web of confusion. As a result, they find themselves feeling trapped in the chaotic and dangerous world of the predator and struggling to save themselves.

**Withholding Information**

Unlike lying, where a predator straight up tells a mistruth to gain something from the other person, withholding information from their victim is used as a way to keep their target at a disadvantage. When a predator withholds information from you, they are doing so with the clear knowledge that you not having this information keeps them at an advantage and ensures that they get exactly what they want from you whether you realize it or not.

For example, say a predator wants you to spend time with their friends, but you want to spend time alone with them. To get their way, a narcissist will invite you out somewhere without telling you that their friends would be present at this gathering, knowing that this would result in you saying "yes" to the invitation. Once you arrived, however, you would see that their friends were all there and that there was never any intention of the two of you spending time alone together. If you attempted to confront the predator on this action, they would simply shrug it off and say something like, "Of course you didn't know they were coming. You never asked." In this case, they are technically right, and it leaves you at a disadvantage because you cannot argue with them – since they are right. However, it is a case of manipulation because they knew full well that you wouldn't ask; therefore, making the fact that they withheld the information both manipulative and cunning.

The best way to arm yourself against this type of predatory behavior is to look for other signs of predatory behavior and then either steer clear of said person or ask plenty of questions. Even if the answers seem obvious, do not be afraid to ask and press for *all* of the information. While this is likely excessive and unnecessary in most relationships, if you have any reason to believe that someone may be manipulating you for their own gain, using this strategy can help you at least attempt to uncover what the truth may be, if you truly need to.

## Mood Swings

Predators are known for having a constant change in their moods, quickly switching between things such as happy and pleased to angry and unsatisfied. While the psychological cause for this is irrelevant, the behavior itself is used as a tool against you to keep you uncertain and at an extreme disadvantage. When you never know what mood the predator will be in, it becomes challenging for you to determine what to expect any time that you are around them. This way, every time you approach them, you are walking on eggshells and doing everything you can to make sure that they are in a good mood and that they stay in a good mood. Based on the lies they tell you, you may be led to believe that your behavior and actions are directly responsible for the constant changes in their moods, even though this has nothing to do with it.

When you find yourself in a situation with a predator and their mood changes, the chances are that they will blame it on you and say something like, "You know I hate when you do that!" as an attempt to make you feel as though it is your fault that they had such a moody reaction to something. In more advanced or attached relationships, this type of behavior is used to make the victim feel as though they are personally responsible for the other person's mood and that they constantly have to behave in a way that pleases the predator. Because they have been entrapped in the predatory manipulation, in many cases, the victim willingly believes this and has little troubles taking responsibility for the mood and actions of the other person, even when these moods result in the victim being hurt in some way.

For the predator, keeping you uncertain and walking on eggshells means that you are constantly off balance and that you are easy to be persuaded and manipulated into believing things that are not true. This is because they are working on the shock factor by eliminating certain clues as to what would upset them or make them unhappy, making it virtually impossible for you to determine when or why their mood will change.

## Love Bombing and Devaluation

Predators, especially ones who are narcissists, use a tool known as "love bombing" and devaluation to manipulate people into falling in love with them and then using this emotion against them. Love bombing is the tactic where a narcissist carefully listens for what you want and need in a partner and then begins to act as though they are the perfect partner for you, leading you to believe that you have hit the romantic jackpot. They will do everything they can to sweep you off your feet, such as bring you gifts, compliment you, make you feel special, and genuinely listen to you (or so it seems.) Everything the narcissist does during the love bombing stage is meant to sweep you off of your feet and put your guard down, while also making you feel as though you are deeply in love with the narcissist; thus creating a deep connection and attachment between the two of you.

Once you have been successfully love-bombed, a narcissist will move into the devaluation phase. This is where they begin to use all of the information that they learned when they were listening to you against you, making you feel as though you are worthless and highlighting your flaws to show you why you are not worthy of love or attention. This experience is extremely painful to a victim, especially since it happens suddenly and without any warning or signals. The narcissist will always blame you for their behavior, saying that the only reason why they are treating you like you are worthless is that you did something wrong to earn the said treatment. They will say things like, "I do everything for you, and this is how you repay me?" allowing them to use their love-bombing stage as a weapon against you, even though you never asked for any of it and everything you gained from the narcissist was openly offered.

This type of behavior is really hard to predict and protect yourself against because, typically, it is done in such a way that it is overwhelming and overstimulates your brain with love chemicals such as oxytocin and dopamine. What ends up happening is that you feel so overwhelmed with love, that when it is ripped away from you during the devaluation stage, you become desperate to get it back and begin taking responsibility for everything just so that you can get back to the dreamy phase of love bombing again. Only, this is exactly what the narcissist wants and expects: this is how they fuel their own need to feel loved and important, by exploiting you and yours.

**Punishment**

Predators are known for constantly punishing people when they do not behave in the "right way". The way a predator punishes someone varies, ultimately depending upon the predator themselves, what has worked for them in the past, and what they feel will work best for them right now at the present moment. Punishments can range between things like the silent treatment or yelling to physical violence and mental abuse, and it is always dealt with the intention of forcing the victim into compliance with them.

The punishment phase with predators can be particularly dangerous because you never truly know what they are capable of or what they will do to you when they choose to begin punishing you. Their punishments are always meant to be scary and overwhelming as this leaves you feeling unsafe and keeps you willing to adhere to almost anything they say or do, anything they want because they can trust that you will not want to provoke them further. As a result, they get everything and anything they want, and you are left begging for forgiveness and doing anything you can to try and restore the peace so that you can stop fearing for your life.

Punishment is not exclusive to close, attached relationships either. This type of predatory behavior is not only something that happens between spouses or family members, despite what many people have been led to believe. This behavior can happen between anyone, but especially when the predator holds a position of power or advantage over the other person. For example, your boss may use punishment as a way to pressure you into taking on more work than is reasonable for your position or salary because they know that you will not risk their job, and they ultimately hold the power to keep you or fire you. Even though they have to adhere to certain legal obligations, a truly manipulative boss knows that you know that they can easily fire you and make it look like it complies with their legal obligations as your boss. This is a perfect example of how anyone can use punishment as a way to exert power over someone else and display a manipulative act of predatory behavior, regardless of the nature of the relationship they share with the other person.

## Denial

If you have ever heard the saying "If you're caught, deny, deny, deny," then you have a pretty good idea of the mindset of predators when it comes to denial. People who are manipulative know that if they never admit to anything, they can never be held accountable for their actions, meaning that they never have to personally endure their rightful consequences. Even if you know that they are guilty of doing something, if they never admit to it, they can begin bending your reality and leading you to believe that you are attempting to commit them when they are actually innocent.

Predators will deny absolutely everything, not only when they fear being caught but just in general. By frequently denying everything, even when they are not being accused of anything, they can not only mitigate responsibility or accountability but also leave you feeling as though you are unable to trust in your own perception or memory. This means that any time they want to lie to you or blame you for something you never truly did, you are already untrusting in yourself and your perception, making it even easier for them to lead you to believe that you truly are at fault, or that what you thought you saw or heard never actually happened.

A key way that predators will use this to their advantage is when you are in public, and you attempt to confront a predator in front of other people. Predators will deny everything you say in front of other people, and they will do so in a way that makes it sound like you are crazy or like you are not a credible source for reliable information. They might say something like, "That never happened. You always forget things like that!" or "There you go, making up stories again." This type of attitude is used to manipulate you while also making others believe that you are a liar so that they also do not believe you; thus making it challenging for you to find someone safe to turn to when you attempt to find safety from your abusive relationship.

## Spinning the Truth

Manipulators and predators are great at spinning the truth to serve their needs. In this way, they are not technically lying, but instead, they are presenting the facts in a way that leads you to see things from their twisted perspective; thus helping them disguise things that they do not want you to know or pick up on. When a manipulative person spins the truth, they will always do so in a way that is subtle and powerful. They may also attempt to overcompensate for the "new truth" as a way to attempt to overwhelm you with facts and information, pressuring you to believe them without critically thinking about anything that they are telling you.

A common area where this is seen is in politics where politicians acknowledge viable facts that are presented to them and then attempt to twist the facts to serve their own agenda. For example, say you confront a politician on a statistic surrounding unemployment by saying something like, "There is still a 45% unemployment rate which is completely unreasonable." A politician using manipulative tactics might say something like, "Yes, we have increased employment to 55% this term," to make it seem as though they have done something positive. In reality, they may have only increased the employment rate by 1%, but because they spin the fact to draw attention away from their shortcomings, they can manipulate people into believing that they are doing a good thing, even if they aren't.

This doesn't only happen in politics. Spinning the truth is a common tactic used by predators, sometimes without any clear intention of what they are seeking to gain from spinning the truth. In some cases, they are simply refining their practice or spinning the truth because they are so used to manipulating others that they cannot have a basic interaction without including tactics like manipulation into the conversation.

## Minimizing

Predators will always attempt to minimize their own actions while maximizing yours, making it seem like what they do is hardly a bad thing and what you do is cruel to the fullest extent. They may also attempt to mitigate their responsibility and minimize their accountability by shifting blame so that you, or someone else, are held accountable for their actions instead of themselves. By doing this, predators make it seem like they truly are not that bad and that the real problem is you, or someone else, who makes them seem like they are bad. In this way, they attempt to victimize themselves so that you stop blaming them and they can constantly get away with anything that they have done.

You can tell that a predator is using the manipulative strategy of minimizing any time you hear them say something like, "Yeah I did that, but it's not as bad as it seems" or "It's not my fault because so and so does it all the time." By saying things like this, they will make it seem as though their own behavior and actions are not as destructive or damaging as they truly are. Most predators have mastered this technique so they can successfully draw attention away from themselves while leaving you feeling as though their actions truly were not that bad, even if they were. As a result, you internalize your anger and find yourself feeling less frustrated towards the manipulator and more frustrated in general, which ultimately supports them in no longer having to take accountability for their actions.

# Playing the Victim

Minimizing their own behaviors while maximizing yours is not the only way that a predator will attempt to play the victim in your shared relationship. There are actually many strategies that manipulators will use to make it seem as though they are the ones who are genuinely being treated wrong or suffering and you are the one responsible for making them suffer. They will use a series of strategies to achieve this, such as lying, spinning the truth, withholding information, minimizing, and denial, each of which is used to make it seem as though they never did anything wrong, but you did. Through this, they create a web of lies that frames you as the bad guy and them as the innocent one, leaving you feeling as though you are at fault and that you need to stop being so harsh to them.

When a manipulative person switches your roles in this way, they can gain sympathy from you and eliminate their need to endure the consequences of their own actions. They are also able to confuse you further and strip you of your own defenses by leaving you feeling completely unclear as to what the true dynamic of the relationship is. Not only does this have you feeling guilty and remorseful for something you likely never did, but it also leaves you feeling like they did nothing wrong *and* that you are unable to trust yourself, your actions, your perception, and your memory.

This behavior can be damaging to experience, but predators make it even more damaging when they include an audience in the experience. By victimizing themselves in public in front of other people, they not only take away your credibility, but they also make it seem like *you* are the one who is hurting *them*. This allows the predator to develop all sorts of toxic emotions within you, from shame to fear, because they know that you will feel guilty for being seen as abusive and that you will become afraid that people will see you as less of a person as a result. Since they know you want to be seen as a good person (and you are a good person), they will attempt to destroy your credibility and trustworthiness through actions like this so that they can isolate you from everyone around you.

## Using Positive Reinforcement

Just like a predator will attempt to use punishment as a way to deter your behaviors and keep you from doing the things that they do not want you to do, they will also use positive reinforcement to condition you to do anything they do want you to do. Positive reinforcement is used as a way to charm you and lead you into believing that they are capable of being positive people, even when the truth is that they are not. Instead, they simply know that this form of flattering behavior will help gloss over the toxic actions they engaged in and divert your attention elsewhere; keeping you focused on how good they make you feel instead of how bad they make you feel.

Some examples of how a manipulator will use positive reinforcement include through constantly apologizing for their behaviors, bringing you gifts and tokens of their appreciation, praising you, excessively charming you, giving you extra attention, or giving you money. When they do things like this, your attention is taken away from the harmful things that they have done and is instead focused on what you stand to gain from the relationship. That way, you are less likely to realize how damaging the relationship truly is and you are more likely to stick around.

These types of positive reinforcements come with two underlying intentions: to increase your love for them, and to condition you into behaving in the way that they specifically want you to behave. When a predator can increase your love for them, they know that you will naturally begin to defend them and justify your reasons for staying with them or around them without ever having to give you any valid reasons. This is based on the basic behavioral law of humans making a decision based on emotions and then justifying their decisions with a biased logic that supports their emotional decision. They also know that you are going to want to experience more positive reinforcement and attention from them, meaning that you will behave in the way they ask you to achieve it. As a result, they get everything they want, and you are left playing the role of their abused puppet, feeding into their manipulative ways without realizing it is even happening.

## Moving the Goal Posts

Manipulative people thrive on remaining unpredictable. When they are unpredictable, there is no way for you to truly know exactly what is going on or what to expect from them, meaning that you are vulnerable to their behaviors. A big way that manipulators will keep you vulnerable is by constantly moving the goal posts, or keeping it unclear as to where you stand with them. If you feel like you have no idea where you stand with a person and your position keeps changing, such as one day you are on positive grounds, and the next you seem to have upset them, you are probably dealing with a predator.

Predators will make it unclear as to where you actually stand with them by consistently switching up the labels they place on your relationship, the way they treat you, or the things that they say about you to other people. For example, they may call you their friend one day, their significant other the next, and their acquaintance the next. Or, they may tell you that you are their significant other and then tell someone else that you are just a friend or that they barely know you. By behaving in this way, predators keep it unclear as to where you stand with them which naturally pressures you into attempting to figure it out. In the pursuit, you do anything you can to try and get the lines clear and attempt to keep the relationship fit within a specific label or position so that you can make sense of the relationship itself. Since they know that you are desperate to figure it out, a manipulator or predator will use this to their advantage by making you jump through hoops and do crazy things just to secure a specific label, only for it to change again just when you thought you had it figured out.

# Diversion

Diversion is the tactic used by predators when they attempt to divert a subject away from their actions or behaviors and instead focus on something else. In this particular strategy, the predator is not actually trying to blame you or highlight your behaviors, but instead, they are simply trying to divert the conversation and focus away from themselves. This is a strategy that they work into their conversations so seamlessly that it seems like the conversation has naturally switched focus, when in reality, they have done it on purpose to cover up their actions and keep themselves blameless.

It is not uncommon for predators to use diversion, even if they are not attempting to hide anything specific or keep you from finding anything out. Instead, they will use it just as a way to keep the conversation away from themselves and focused on other things. By doing this, they can avoid having to recall the lies they have told, potentially say something that contradicts something they have already said or otherwise do something that could lead to them needing to cover their trail. This is often a lazy behavior used by predators as a way to try and cover up the truth when they are simply too lazy to cover it up should they accidentally expose a part of their web.

Another reason why predators might do this is if they do not feel as though they have anything significant to gain from a conversation, or if they are trying to gain information from someone else to use at a later point. For example, if they are in a conversation with someone new and they do not know what to brag about or how to make themselves look good in front of the said person, they may divert the conversation away from themselves so that the new person can talk. Through this, they can accumulate information about this new person and plot their strategy to earn this person's trust or affection and then twist it against them; thus making them a new victim of the predator's behavior.

## Sarcasm

Sarcasm is a common tactic that is used to throw victims off balance and keep predators looking smart and credible. One big way that a predator will use sarcasm is by being sarcastic about or towards a victim in front of other people; thus helping them lower the self-esteem and self-confidence of their victim and showing off how powerful they are. Common sentences used by predators include things like, "Yeah, stupid, that's exactly what they meant" or "No kidding." These small jabs hold great power in making a victim feel an even lower sense of self-esteem, further damaging their ability to fight back or defend themselves against the predator.

In personal conversations, sarcasm is often used as a way to cover up lies or hide information that the predator does not want the victim to know about. For example, if you think back to the story about Thomas Edison and Nicola Tesla, you might recall the part of the story where Edison offers Tesla $50,000 to complete a job. Once Tesla completes the job, Edison uses sarcasm to cover up the fact that he had no intention of ever paying Tesla $50,000 in exchange for his services by laughing and saying, "You don't understand American humor!" This was a form of sarcasm used to cover up the fact that Edison made an offer he was never actually going to follow through on, leaving Tesla feeling humiliated and as though he had made a mistake and not instead been cheated in a bogus deal.

## Guilt Tripping

Guilt tripping their victims is a way that predators can make their victims feel personally responsible for the way they have been treated based on something they have done either in general or to the manipulator themselves. Guilt tripping allows a predator to lead a victim into believing that they are mean, maniacal, or abusive towards others. This leads the victim into feeling as though they have done something wrong and they need to change or become more aware of their behaviors to avoid hurting those around them.

Often, the guilt trip is laced with validation that is derived from actions that have been spun to make it seem as though the victim was being intentionally mean, when in reality, they weren't.

For example, say you are out with friends, and a friend spills coffee on their shirt, and you laugh at them for their misfortune, knowing that they are also laughing at themselves, even if they seem frustrated or angry at that moment. In reality, this is simply a funny experience, and your friend likely does not care that you are laughing at them for what happened. However, a predator may lead you into believing that laughing at your friend when they spilled coffee was abusive and that you humiliated your friend and made them not like you any longer. They may use the fact that you haven't talked in several days as proof that this person does not like you, even if it is natural for your relationship to go through ebbs and flows of talking a lot and then not talking so much. Because you are being guilt-tripped, you begin to believe that you are in fact a destructive person and that you hurt those in your life, such as the manipulator who is likely claiming that you have in some way hurt them, even if you haven't.

This type of behavior leads to you feeling hyper-aware of everything you do and attempting to make up for it by developing a deep sense of self-consciousness. By staying fixated on every single action you make and second-guessing everything you do, you attempt to avoid hurting other people through your "destructive ways". In reality, you likely never hurt anyone in the first place, but now, your self-esteem is lowered, and your sense of perception is altered, so once again, you are at the mercy of the manipulator and their deceptive ways.

# Flattery

Predators love using flattery and charm as a way to gain people's trust and earn their respect. Typically, predators are very charming towards everyone they meet as this allows them to be seen as kind, nice, and trustworthy. This also ensures that no one suspects them for being a predator; thus leaving them able to do anything they want without anyone ever suspecting them because they are "too nice" to do such a thing. A predator will do this to everyone, including to their victim, as this ensures that they stay on the positive side of everyone's emotional radar which leaves them free to do whatever they want without ever being suspected as predators.

If you find that someone seems to be complimenting you more than normal or they seem excessively interested in finding reasons to compliment you in ways that stand out from the standard compliment, beware. These are the typical actions of a predator who is trying to make you feel special and unique so that they can wreak havoc on your mental state for their own personal gain. Even if it feels positive, be cautious and keep your guard up around this person until it becomes very clear that you are safe around them and that they will not hurt you. Even still, be ready to pay attention to other common behaviors of a predator, such as love bombing and devaluing, to ensure that you do not get sucked into their wrath.

## Playing Innocent

Manipulators are masters at faking their emotions and doing so with such grace that it is virtually impossible to tell if they are being truthful or not. In masterfully faking their emotions and hiding their true feelings and expressions, a manipulator can easily cover over their wrongdoings with expressions of shock, confusion, and defensiveness. When a manipulator plays the victim card, they will do so in a way that is so seamless that the true victim genuinely believes their reaction and begins to question whether or not their accusations are actually founded.

One way that a manipulator can further increase their ability to play the victim card is by keeping their acts of manipulation and abuse extremely subtle yet highly effective. For example, spinning the truth does not mean that they actually lied, but instead, they used the truth to their advantage to bend the reality of their victim. Then, when their victim attempts to call them out on this and state that it was done intentionally, the manipulator plays the victim card and pretends that they are surprised and hurt that the victim would ever think such a thing. This leads to the victim wondering if the action of spinning the truth was intentional and done maliciously or if it was a mistake or that it didn't even happen at all.

Manipulators know that if they react to accusations with shock and surprise, they will subconsciously pressure the true victim into feeling bad and attempting to make up for "attacking" the manipulator. In reality, no attack had ever happened because the victim was merely calling the manipulator out on their malicious behavior. However, because the victim believes the manipulator's surprised reaction, they begin feeling guilty for accusing the manipulator, and so they start trying to make up for their "false" accusations. In the end, the manipulator's tracks are covered and the victim never truly gets to the bottom of the manipulative tactics that were used against them.

## Excessive Aggression

Aggression is an anxiety-inducing behavior that can cause anyone who isn't expressing aggression to feel fearful and unsafe. Manipulators are known for using excessive amounts of aggression as a way to shock their victims and force them into a state of submission. When a manipulative person becomes aggressive, their actions and behaviors become unpredictable which leaves those around them feeling unsafe and uncertain as to what they should expect from the manipulator. The manipulator themselves are likely bluffing with aggression as a way to get what they want, but in some cases, the aggression goes so far as to cause serious physical harm to those around them. This is especially common in narcissists, psychopaths, and sociopaths who have no empathy and who appear to have no capacity to stop themselves from hurting anyone – since they do not feel the consequences of their hurtful behaviors.

When a victim, especially a long-time victim, is exposed to the aggressive behaviors of the manipulator, they will immediately comply with anything that the manipulator asks for because they want to end the aggressive behaviors. This is the victim's only way of truly knowing that they are safe from the aggression. The manipulator recognizes this and knows that aggression makes their victim compliant, so they will use it any time they want their victim to comply. With some manipulators, aggression is used as a last resort when their other manipulative behaviors are not working, and they are feeling as though they are losing control. With others, it is used frequently as a way to rattle the victim and keep them uncertain and fearful so that they never truly know what to expect.

Another reason why manipulators use anger is to attempt to end conversations quickly and without any questions asked. When a manipulative person becomes excessively angry during a conversation, in many cases, they are doing so to attempt to end the conversation so that their victim becomes confused. This takes away focus from the original conversation topic and puts the victim into the state of trying to control the aggressor's anger; thus helping them bury the original topic and preserve themselves from being "caught". In this scenario, the victim recalls that attempting to press for more information on the original subject led to a terrifying experience with the manipulator, meaning that they are less likely to press for answers or question the manipulator on that subject again.

## Isolation

Predators will always attempt to isolate a victim so that they are easier to control. You may recognize this from counts of sexual predators in the news, where they typically use isolated victims as their targets because there is no one to prevent them from taking action. For example, a girl on her way to the bathroom by herself or who is walking home alone in the dark. These are excellent targets for sexual predators who want to take advantage of someone to fulfill their own sick and twisted desires. Sexual predators are not the only ones who will use isolation as a form of manipulation, however, to help them get what they want. Virtually any manipulative person will use this as a strategy to try and get their way because they know that it is easier to convince and manipulate one person than many. This is why young children who are just learning how to get what they want will go ask only one parent – the more giving parent – when they want something that they suspect their parents will say "no" to. In a child's case, however, most times, they are simply young, and this is a phase that can be corrected by parents upon witnessing this behavior. In adults or children who have not learned that this type of behavior is wrong, this type of manipulative behavior is used as a way to get what they want from others.

Using the isolation technique works best when a person wants to do something malicious and does not want an audience who could potentially prevent them from achieving the said thing. In abusive relationships, this might look like slowly isolating their victim from all of their friends and family by making their loved ones think that they are crazy liars who are abusing the manipulative person and not the other way around. In the workplace, this may look like your boss waiting for you to be by yourself before approaching you to attempt to pressure you into doing something like taking on more work than is reasonable for your position. Amongst your friends, this can look like one friend trying to isolate you to attempt to recruit you into doing something malicious or unkind towards the other friend, such as ditch them or play a mean joke on them. There are many ways that this behavior can be used to attempt to manipulate unwanted behavior out of a person. This is because manipulators know that when someone is isolated, they feel a greater sense of fear in saying "no" because there is no one to protect them from the wrath of the manipulator. If the victim already knows what the manipulator is capable of, this fear grows even larger because they are worried that not complying with the manipulator could lead to serious negative consequences. By keeping their victim isolated, the manipulator can easily bend the reality of their victim and pressure them into doing anything they want without the victim feeling like there is any other option to protect them.

# They Fake Love and Empathy

True predators who are known to be psychopaths, sociopaths, or narcissists do not know how to experience love or empathy for anyone except for themselves. This is why they can partake in Machiavellian power tactics without feeling any sense of remorse or guilt for their actions: because they genuinely believe that everyone else is a bad person and that they are a victim of the entire world. From this mentality, they can emotionally and mentally isolate themselves from everyone else and employ a "me versus all of you" mentality. This is why they feel absolutely no remorse for hurting those around them and using others as pawns in their ploy to generate more power from those around them. To them, everyone else is a horrible person, and they deserve the pain being caused upon them by the manipulator.

Even though this is the true mentality of a predator, they will never let anyone around them believe that this is how they genuinely think and feel. That is because predators know that other people thrive on having empathy and love in their lives and they all genuinely believe in these two things and share them freely with those around them. By faking signs of love and empathy for others, predators can blend in with general society and begin wreaking havoc on anyone they please to because they know that they can go undetected this way.

When a predator is showing empathy or love for those around them, what they are actually doing is mirroring what they see in others. Their empathy and love are completely fake, and the ways they are showing it are based on the interactions they have seen take place between others and not based on the genuine feelings that they have within themselves. For this reason, no love or empathy is genuinely felt by a predator towards anyone else, which is what makes it so easy for them to take on victims and do cruel and unthinkable things to them.

# Chapter 7: Deceptive Winners

When it comes to people who are practicing using Machiavellian power, they always have one solitary goal: to win. They want everything they want, and they refuse to ever settle for any less than what they desire. In many people, this type of determined quality is positive and can lead to them putting in the work to achieve their desired results and being happy with the positive outcome that they get. With Machiavellians and people who use dark psychology, this type of determination means that they will stop at nothing to win and they are not afraid to take immoral steps to achieve their success.

Four main tactics allow deception to step into the art of winning in a way that lets Machiavellian people win at anything they do. These include deceiving others about their true resources, deceiving people into believing in their strategies, using deception as part of a bigger plan, and deceptively covering their tracks so they cannot be caught. Deception is a major power tool that is used by Machiavellians so that they can use their immoral winning tactics and get away with them without ever having anyone clearly blame them for their manipulative strategies. In this chapter, we are going to discover how Machiavellian leaders use these tactics to get their way in virtually every situation.

## Deceive People about your Resources

Most people who are attempting to settle negotiations or win something will do so by being honest about their resources and then creatively using their resources to produce the desired results of both parties. This is how they can stay honorable while also being able to achieve a successful deal between themselves and those around them. For example, say a politician wanted to win an election but wanted to do so in a way that stayed honest to their resources and capabilities. In their campaigning, this politician would be honest about what they are truly capable of achieving and what resources they have to support them, and then they would propose solutions to their voters that were honestly capable of achieving their voter's desired results. This type of campaigning is honest and transparent and gives the voters a realistic sense of what can be achieved and how.

For someone who is willing to win using Machiavellian powers, however, they will bring deception into the practice and start deceiving the voters to attempt to lure them into believing that the politician can do more than they truly can. However, the deceptive winner will never say specifically what they will achieve in office. Instead, they will provide ideas and proposals. As they are offering these ideas and proposals, deceptive politicians will word them in a way that makes it sound like they will *absolutely* make it happen, but will include small nuances that allow them to backtrack at a later date. This way, when they are asked questions after winning, such as "You said you would make *x* happen, when will it happen?" they can say something like, "I never said that I *would* make it happen; I said that I *would try.*" When the voters go back and look at the footage of their campaigns, they will realize that various word plays were thrown into the conversation that made it clear that they were being untrue but that was masterfully hidden during the live conversation itself. This way, the politician is not technically lying, and the individuals confronting them cannot find solid grounds to argue from, so they are unable to truly convict the politician of lying. Instead, the politician has successfully deceived everyone into believing them so that they could win the election. Once they have won, it is too late for the voters to do anything to reverse the actions.

When a person uses deception to hide their resources, they are trying to ensure that everyone believes in their capabilities, but no one truly sees that they do not have the means to achieve their proposed promises. As a result, they can win their deceptive games with a large group of supporters who are unable to *technically* pinpoint the wrongdoing of the deceptive winner, so they struggle to determine whether their actions were untrue or not.

## Deceive People into Believing in your Strategy

When a Machiavellian leader cannot deceive people into believing in their resources, they will move on to deceive them into believing in their strategy instead. Or, sometimes, they will combine both types of deception to create a massive web of lies and confusion that keeps their supporters on board with their mission. By deceiving people into believing that they have a great strategy that can be used to achieve a common goal, manipulative leaders can gain followers who support in their cause, even though their cause is far from honest or achievable.

The key tactic that a manipulator will use to achieve someone's support when they are trying to win something is fear mongering. Fear mongering means to instill messages of fear into those around them and fill their heads with beliefs that they are in danger or that if action is not taken, something terrible will happen. This type of behavior is known as "psychological warfare" and coincides with other forms of psychological warfare such as isolating, victim-blaming, love bombing, and other manipulative behaviors.

Once people are afraid, they are filled with fear and are immediately searching for ways to protect themselves against that which they fear. This makes them far more agreeable when it comes to listening to their Machiavellian leader's proposal and believing in it because, at that point, they are not thinking rationally and they are ready to do anything they can to protect themselves.

A great example of this in recent history is Donald Trump's proposal to build a wall between the United States of America and Mexico. Realistically, a wall would be unlikely to keep anyone out if they truly wanted to get in; they would simply find another way to enter the country illegally and continue doing what they were doing all along. Furthermore, the fear mongering allowed Trump to cover up the fact that illegal immigrants are not a large of an issue as he made them out to be, nor were they the most prominent issue that the country was facing at the time. However, Trump knew that this was a very real concern for the population of job seekers who were struggling to land jobs and he knew that by instilling a fear that they would never land jobs so long as immigrants continued coming into the country, he could gain their support. Through this, his momentum grew, and he was able to magnify the problem and draw a lot of attention through this isolated issue. Even though Trump did not have the resources to put the wall up, he did make it seem as though he had the strategy to get it put up anyway: force the Mexican government into putting it up. Because he had instilled so much fear in his supporters, people believed that his strategy would work and stood behind him 100%.

## Deception Is a Tool Not a Plan

People who are trying to win through deception know that deception itself is not the entire plan, but instead, it is a tool that is used to make the larger plan happen. If a deceptive winner were to rely solely on deception as a plan, their plan would quickly fall through as people would notice that they were using deception – since it would likely be used too much. Furthermore, it would prevent them from being able to achieve success because they would have no clear direction as to where they were going or what they were actually doing to achieve success in their chosen direction.

Instead of using deception as a primary plan in winning, Machiavellian leaders will use it as a tool to help cover up the real plan and keep them from getting caught. This way, a manipulative leader can be working on the real plan behind the scenes while their entire following remains oblivious to the goings-on of the leader. Any time they are brought into the spotlight for their true motivations, they will simply use more deception to cover up their tracks and avoid being caught. If deception itself stops working, true manipulators will have plenty of other tools to fall back on to support them in keeping their following strong and supportive. For example, sparking strong emotions within their following and then manipulating their emotions to use them as a tool to keep their followers loyal and on board.

A Machiavellian leader or deceptive winner knows that if their opponent uncovers their deception, it can quickly be used against them to blow up their entire ability to achieve success. This is why they use deception sparingly and mix it with genuine and honest offers, often ones that are laced with other manipulative tactics like spinning the truth or inspiring specific emotions in their audience that supports them in believing the manipulator's deception. They will also produce and maintain a cover story any time they use deception so that they can avoid being caught. By giving a bogus reason to their deceptive actions, they can make it seem as though they were being genuine and honorable, and avoid having their audience turn on them; thus causing them to lose the support they require to win. Deception is merely a tool that is used to help them move forward with their plan, not the entire plan itself.

## Use Deception to Cover your Tracks

When a Machiavellian leader uses deception to win, they will always do so in a way that blends together facts and fiction so that their entire deceptive strategy is not a lie. This way, they can cover their tracks and avoid being seen as truly deceptive: because they know that if anyone were to attempt to uncover their deception, they could simply draw attention to the areas where they were telling the truth. This way, it seems as though the entire statement was the truth, even though it was never honest and it had deceptive intentions.

Using misinformation and decoys can consume your opponent with fear and leave them coming back to you for more information or seeing you as the ultimate authority. This is a common strategy that is used when it comes to trying to win any form of battle or competition between Machiavellian leaders.

A great example of where deception was used to cover tracks and hide intention was in the invasion of Normandy during World War II. In this war, the allies (Great Britain, the United States, China, and the Soviet Union) used deception as a way to paralyze Hitler's attempts and leave him confused and uncertain as to what they were going to do to stop him from his malicious mission. Because fake armies and lookalikes were constantly deceiving him, he never truly knew what to do, and so his reaction rates were massively slowed down. As a result, he struggled to know where to focus his energy and what the actual threats were against his people. Eventually, this deception resulted in him and his military losing the war.

Hitler wasn't only a victim of deception, either, during this war. He also began using deception as a way to help him succeed in creating a fake army to use as a decoy for when the allies invaded Normandy on D-Day. Since he had no idea where the allies would actually land, he made large blow-up versions of tanks and cannons and placed them on various areas across the beach. From close up, these items were clearly fake, but from far away, they looked extremely real. This meant that when the allies landed, they would be attempting to protect themselves against a fake army while Hitler's real army was hidden a short distance away, ready to fight against the allies. In World War II, deception was a major tactic used to attempt to deceive the opposing army so that each side could win. In the end, the allies won, and Hitler's army was stopped from wreaking havoc on the world.

# Conclusion

This book should have given you some strong insight into how Machiavellian leaders and manipulative people take advantage of others to fulfill their own twisted fantasies in life. Being taken advantage of and getting dragged into the dark psychology of manipulative people is never enjoyable, but unfortunately, it happens to people on a regular basis by understanding what deceptive strategies look like and how manipulative people use manipulation, mind control, deception, persuasion, negotiation, human behavior, and psychological warfare to get their way in life. While we all want to achieve our dreams and live out our fantasies, some people are willing to go to shameless extents to achieve their goals and fulfill their dreams. Often, they hurt many people along the way and show no remorse or consideration for the pain that they have caused.

Machiavellian leaders and predators can be so good at what they do that you have no idea that you are actually being manipulated into becoming a pawn that is used to help them in fulfilling their fantasies. Because of their extensive selection of tools and dark psychological strategies, they can deceive you into believing that everything they do is honest and genuine and you are the crazy one for not believing in them and their causes. By taking away your self-confidence and the trust you have in yourself, a Machiavellian leader can ensure that you never question their judgment or actions and that you stay true to them as you stray away from your own moral compass. This makes it even easier for them to keep you entangled in their twisted scheming so that you can support them in winning their game of life.

If you have ever been manipulated by someone in your life, the chances are that you have witnessed these very behaviors taking place between yourself and another human. By reading this book and getting a solid understanding of what these behaviors look like and how they are used against healthy unsuspecting people, you can better protect yourself from future manipulative attempts. If manipulation has been a problem for you in your life, keeping this book handy may support you in recalling various deceptive tools that manipulators use to victimize others. That way, you can avoid being dragged into deception and manipulation again in the future.

Remember, this book was in no way written to endorse deceptive behaviors or encourage you to begin manipulating those around you to try and get your way in life. Dark psychology is a dangerous tactic to use, and in many cases, the person using the dark psychology will lose simply because this is a destructive and cruel strategy for getting what you want. Even if it seems like an easy way to win, it truly is not, and it can destroy your life in some of the worst ways. People who live this way often lack true love and empathy in their lives, which can be a sad and painful way to exist in this world. Avoid using these traits as a way to get what you want. Instead, focus on being honest and maintaining your integrity while avoiding people who use these types of behaviors for their own benefit. That is how you can truly win.

Lastly, if you enjoyed this book and it helped give you a deeper look and understanding into the mindset of manipulators, deceivers, and abusers, please leave a review on Amazon. Your honest feedback would be greatly appreciated.

# Check out another book by Steven Turner

Printed in Poland
by Amazon Fulfillment
Poland Sp. z o.o., Wrocław